# 2 Longman Academic Writing Series

THIRD EDITION

## PARAGRAPHS

Ann Hogue

with Jennifer Bixby

**Longman Academic Writing Series 2: Paragraphs, Third Edition**



Pearson Education, 221 River Street, Hoboken, NJ 07030

**Staff Credits:** The people who made up the ***Longman Academic Writing Series 2*** team, representing editorial, production, design, and manufacturing, are Pietro Alongi, Margaret Antonini, Eleanor Barnes, Stephanie Bullard, Kim Casey, Tracey Cataldo, Aerin Csigay, Ann France, Shelley Gazes, Pam Kirshen-Fishman, Amy McCormick, Lise Minovitz, Liza Pleva, Joan Poole, Robert Ruvo, and Joseph Vella.

Cover image: jupeart/Shutterstock
Text Composition: TSI Graphics

**Library of Congress Cataloging-in-Publication Data**

Hogue, Ann.
[First steps in academic writing]
Longman Academic Writing Series, Level 2: Paragraphs / Ann Hogue, Jennifer Bixby.—Third edition.
pages cm.—(Longman Academic Writing Series)
ISBN-13: 978-0-13-291271-6
ISBN-10: 0-13-291271-6
1. English language—Rhetoric. 2. Academic writing. I. Bixby, Jennifer. II. Title
PE1478.H57 2013
808'.042—dc23

2012046182

ISBN 10: 0-13-466333-0
ISBN 13: 978-0-13-466333-3

Printed in the United States of America
18 2019

# CONTENTS

## Appendices

# TO THE TEACHER

Welcome to the new edition of Level 2 in the *Longman Academic Writing Series*, a five-level series that prepares learners of English for academic coursework. This book, formerly called *First Steps in Academic Writing*, is intended for high-beginning students in a university, college, or secondary program. It offers a carefully structured approach that focuses on writing as a process. It teaches rhetoric and sentence structure in a straightforward manner, using a step-by-step approach, high-interest models, and varied practice types.

Like the previous editions, this text integrates instruction in paragraph organization, sentence structure, grammar, and mechanics with the writing process. It carefully guides students through the steps of the writing process to produce the well-organized, clearly developed paragraphs that are essential to academic writing in English. Realistic models guide students, and clear explanations supported by examples help them through typical rough spots. These explanations are followed by extensive practice that helps students assimilate writing skills and write with accuracy and confidence. These practice activities include interactive tasks such as pair and group work to round out the solitary work of individual writing. They progress from recognition exercises to controlled production exercises to communicative Try It Out activities, which serve to engage students in the process of their own learning.

Each of its six chapters focuses on a standard pattern of paragraph organization and culminates in a final carefully staged writing assignment. The first three chapters focus on personal topics which gradually give way to the more academic topics and genres of the latter half of the book. Finally, the appendices and a thorough index reinforce student learning and serve as useful reference guides.

## What's New in This Edition

Instructors familiar with the second edition will find these new features:

- **Chapter objectives** provide clear goals for instruction;
- **Two new vocabulary sections**, *Looking at Vocabulary* and *Applying Vocabulary*, explain vocabulary from the writing models and support its use in the *Writing Assignment*;
- Selected **writing models** have been updated or replaced, while old favorites have been retained and improved;
- **Prewriting** and **outlining** sections have been expanded and improved;
- **Self-Assessments** ask students to evaluate their own progress;
- **Timed Writing** practices develop students' writing fluency.

## The Online Teacher's Manual

The Teacher's Manual is available at **www.pearsonELT.com/tmkeys**. It includes general teaching notes, chapter teaching notes, answer keys, reproducible writing assignment scoring rubrics, and reproducible chapter quizzes.

## Acknowledgments

Many people have helped shape the third edition of this book. First and foremost, Jennifer Bixby brought tireless dedication to this book and contributed many new models, practices, activities, and assignments.

Members of the Pearson ELT team, particularly Amy McCormick, Lise Minovitz, and Eleanor Kirby Barnes, brought their expertise and dedication to this project. Diane Flanel Piniaris also contributed her time, support, and guidance in developing this book.

Thanks to the many users of the first and second editions of this book who took the time to offer suggestions: **Sandy Abouda**, Seminole Community College, Florida; **Linda Betan**, Columbus State University, Georgia; **Vicki Blaho,** Santa Monica College, California; **Jeff Cady**, College of Marin, California; **Eileen Cotter**, Montgomery College, Maryland; **Jackye Cumby**, Mercer University, Georgia; **Greg Davis**, Portland State University, Oregon; **Diana Davidson del Toro**, Cuyamaca College, California; **Terry Eisele**, Columbus State Community College, Ohio; **Diane Harris**, Imperial Valley College, California, **Mohammed Iqbal**, City College of San Francisco, California; **Linda Lieberman**, College of Marin, California; **Kathleen May**, Howard Community College, Maryland; **Mark Neville**, ALHOSN University, Abu Dhabi, United Arab Emirates; **Kim Sano**, Aoyama Gakuin Women's Junior College, Japan; **Laura Shier**, Portland State University, Oregon; **Christine Tierney**, Houston Community College, Texas.

Thanks also to the following people for their feedback on our online survey: **Eric Ball**, Langara College, British Columbia, Canada; **Mongi Baratli**, Al Hosn University, Abu Dhabi, United Arab Emirates; **Jenny Blake**, Culture Works ESL, London, Canada; **Karen Blinder**, English Language Institute, University of Maryland, Maryland; **Bob Campbell**, Academic Bridge Program, Doha, Qatar; **Nancy Epperson**, Truman College, Illinois; **Kemal Erkol**, Onsekiz Mart University, Çanakkale, Turkey; **Russell Frank**, Pasadena City College, California; **Jeanne Gross**, Cañada College, California; **Lisa Kovacs-Morgan**, English Language Institute, University of California at San Diego, California; **Mary Ann T. Manatlao**, Qatar Foundation, Academic Bridge Program, Doha, Qatar; **Ruth Moore**, University of Colorado at Boulder, Colorado; **Brett Reynolds**, Humber Institute of Technology and Advanced Learning, Ontario, Canada; **Lorraine C. Smith**, CUNY Queens College, New York.

*—Ann Hogue*

# CHAPTER OVERVIEW

*Longman Academic Writing Series, Level 2, Paragraphs* offers a carefully structured approach to high-beginning academic writing. It features instruction on paragraph organization, sentence structure, grammar, mechanics, and the writing process.

**Four-color design** makes the lessons even more engaging.

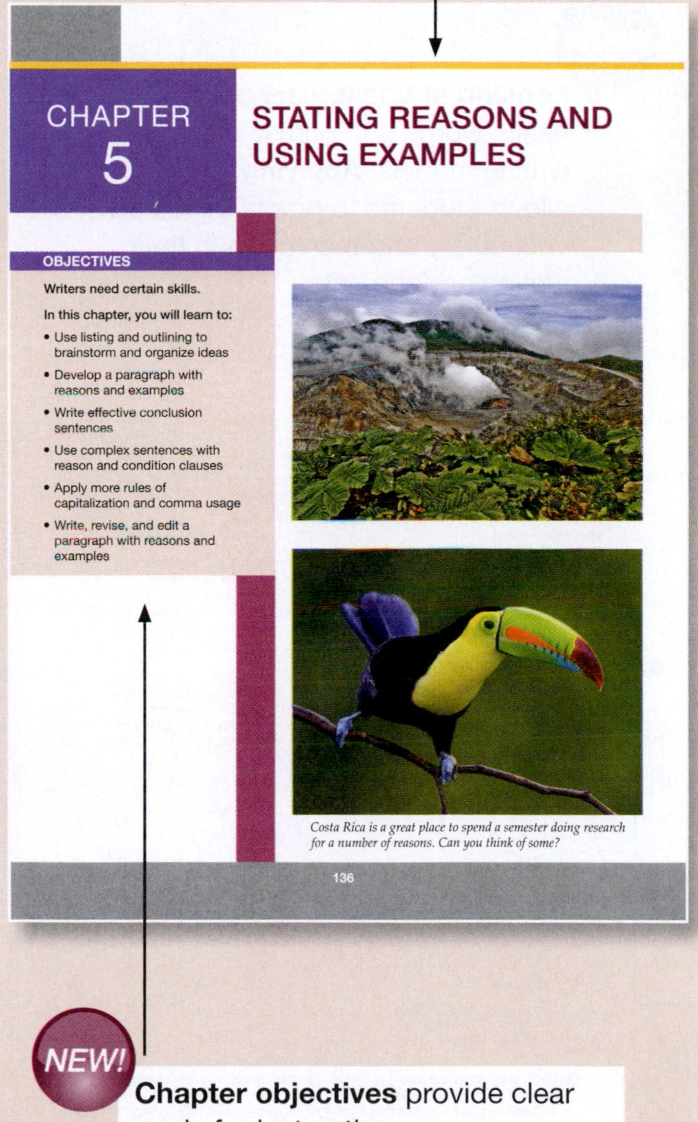

CHAPTER 5

STATING REASONS AND USING EXAMPLES

OBJECTIVES

Writers need certain skills.

In this chapter, you will learn to:

- Use listing and outlining to brainstorm and organize ideas
- Develop a paragraph with reasons and examples
- Write effective conclusion sentences
- Use complex sentences with reason and condition clauses
- Apply more rules of capitalization and comma usage
- Write, revise, and edit a paragraph with reasons and examples

*Costa Rica is a great place to spend a semester doing research for a number of reasons. Can you think of some?*

136

NEW!

**Chapter objectives** provide clear goals for instruction.

**Prewriting** sections introduce students to such techniques as clustering, freewriting, listing, and outlining.

INTRODUCTION

You learned in Chapter 1 that a paragraph is a group of sentences about one topic. A paragraph should have three main parts: a topic sentence, supporting sentences (the body), and a concluding sentence.

In this chapter, you will study each of these parts in more detail. You will also work with and then write paragraphs that use an organization pattern known as listing order. Then you will learn about compound sentences to help you combine your ideas more effectively.

To help you get ideas for your paragraphs, you will first do some prewriting.

PREWRITING

There are many different prewriting techniques that you can use to get ideas to write about. In this chapter you will use clustering.

CLUSTERING

**Clustering** is a prewriting technique that allows you to brainstorm and develop your ideas with the help of a diagram called a **cluster**. Here is how to do it.

Begin by writing your topic in the middle of your paper. Draw a circle around it. Then think of ideas related to the topic. Write words or short phrases in circles around the topic and connect them with lines to the main circle. Write down every idea that comes into your mind. Don't stop to worry if an idea is a good one or not.

CLUSTER 1

Listing-Order Paragraphs 35

**Realistic writing models** present the type of writing students will learn to produce in the end-of-chapter Writing Assignments.

## LOOKING AT THE MODEL

The writing model describes a lecture hall at a community college. As you read, notice how the writer carefully moves his focus from one location to another around the room.

**Work with a partner or in a small group. Read the model. Then answer the questions.**

Writing Model

### The New Lecture Hall

Our community college's beautiful new lecture hall is spacious, modern, and comfortable. On the front wall, there is a large white screen. Instructors can use this for projecting overhead transparencies, slide shows, and audiovisual presentations. Behind the screen, there is a huge whiteboard. To the left of the screen is a clock, and underneath the clock are the light switches. There are two black leather armchairs against the wall. At the front of the lecture hall is the instructor's desk. It's very modern and curved, and it's made of beautiful wood. It looks elegant, in fact. In the center of the desk, there is an overhead projector, and next to it is a computer. To the right of the desk is a lectern. Some instructors like to stand at the lectern and talk. In the main part of the lecture hall, in front of the teacher's desk, there are about 30 rows of seats for students. The black seats are cushioned, so they are comfortable to sit on during long lectures. On the left of each seat, there is a small folding tabletop. Students can use these when they want something to write on. There's also 3 feet of space between the rows, so students have room to stretch their legs. To sum up, our new lecture hall is a pleasing and comfortable place to learn.

**Questions about the Model**

1. Does the topic sentence create a positive or negative impression of the lecture hall?
2. Which space order does the writer use to describe the lecture hall: clockwise, front to back, back to front, or top to bottom?
3. The writer describes three main areas of the lecture hall. What are they?

Describing with Space Order 111

NEW!

**Looking at Vocabulary** points out useful words and phrases from the writing models. **Applying Vocabulary** allows students to practice the new vocabulary and then use it in their writing assignments.

### Looking at Vocabulary: Prepositions of Place

When you write a description of a place, you will often use words and phrases starting with prepositions to describe where things are.

**In the back of the room** is a large white cabinet. There's a clock **above the cabinet**.

You may already know the meaning of many prepositions, but a challenge that all learners face is to use them accurately. For example, it's easy to confuse *in*, *on*, and *at*. It's also common for learners to have trouble knowing whether to use *in front of* or *at the front of*. Noticing the details of these phrases will allow you to use them more accurately.

**PRACTICE 2** Looking at Prepositions of Place

**A** Look at objects 1–10. Circle the first mention of each of these in the writing model on page 111, and underline the phrase that describes where it is. Then use the underlined words to complete phrases in the second column.

| Objects | Location |
|---|---|
| 1. large white screen | ___on___ the front wall |
| 2. huge whiteboard | ______ the screen |
| 3. clock | ______ the screen |
| 4. light switches | ______ the clock |
| 5. armchairs | ______ the wall |
| 6. instructor's desk | ______ the lecture hall |
| 7. lectern | ______ the desk |
| 8. 30 rows of seats | ______ the teacher's desk |
| 9. small folding tabletop | ______ each seat |
| 10. 3 feet of space | ______ the rows |

**B** Think about the location of five things in your classroom. On a separate sheet of paper, write a clue to describe where each thing is. Use five different prepositions from Part A. Begin each sentence with *It's* or *They're*.

1. It's under Mr. Brown's desk.
2. They're on the wall.

Then read your clues to a partner and ask him or her to guess what you are describing.

112 CHAPTER 4

**Practice activities** reinforce learning and lay the groundwork for the end-of-chapter Writing Assignment.

**Organization** sections explore paragraph format and structure in a variety of organizational patterns.

## ORGANIZATION

In Chapter 1, you learned that a paragraph has three parts: a topic sentence, supporting sentences, and a concluding sentence. Now you will study each part of a paragraph in more detail.

### THE TOPIC SENTENCE

The most important sentence in a paragraph is the **topic sentence**. It is called the topic sentence because it tells readers what the main idea of the paragraph is. In other words, it tells readers what they are going to read about. The topic sentence is usually the first sentence in a paragraph. It is the top piece of bread in our paragraph "sandwich."

A topic sentence has two parts: 1) a **topic**, which tells what the paragraph will be about, and 2) a **controlling idea**, which tells what the paragraph will say about the topic. It tells the reader: This paragraph will discuss these things—and only these things—about this topic.

For example, the topic of the writing model on page 38 is *good flight attendants*. What will the paragraph say about good flight attendants? The controlling idea tells us: *They have three important characteristics*. The paragraph will not talk about their uniforms, their training, or their duties. It will only discuss three important characteristics that good flight attendants have.

Here are examples of topic sentences about English:

English is constantly adding new words.

English borrows words from other languages.

English is necessary for many different jobs.

Note that the topic in each of these examples is the same (*English*), but the controlling ideas are different. That means that each paragraph will discuss something very different about English.

40 CHAPTER 2

**Simple explanations** and **clear examples** enable students to improve their grasp of paragraph structure and organization.

### CONCLUSION SIGNALS

In addition to the conclusion signals such as *Indeed* and *To sum up* that you have already learned (see Chapter 2, page 53), you can begin a concluding sentence with *For these (two/three/four) reasons* and *Because of ______*. Notice these two patterns:

PATTERN 1: **For these ______ reasons,** (+ *sentence*).

**For these two reasons,** Costa Rica is a wonderful place to study if you love wildlife.

PATTERN 2: **Because of** (*noun phrase*), (+ *sentence*).

**Because of its diverse habitats and many animal species,** Costa Rica is a wonderful place to study if you love wildlife.

**PRACTICE 8** Using Conclusion Signals

**A** Look back at the outline in Part A of Practice 5, page 145. Use *Indeed* or *To sum up*, *For these ______ reasons*, and *Because of ______* to rewrite the concluding sentence in three different ways.

1. *Indeed, if you're looking for great food, amazing service, and reasonable prices, Joe's Diner is the place to go.*
2. ______
3. ______

**B** Look back at the outline in Part B of Practice 5, page 146. Write three different conclusions, using *Indeed* or *To sum up*, *For these ______ reasons*, and *Because of ______*.

1. ______
2. ______
3. ______

**TRY IT OUT!** Write a paragraph recommending a place to study English using the outline you created in Practice 1 (page 139). Follow these directions.

1. Follow your outline as you write your draft.
2. Use transition signals to introduce your reasons and examples. Try to use *for example*, *for instance*, and *such as* at least once.
3. Add a concluding sentence. Remember to use an appropriate conclusion signal, such as *Indeed*, *To sum up*, *For ______ reasons*, or *Because of ______*.
4. Proofread your paragraph, and correct any mistakes.

150 CHAPTER 5

NEW!

**Try It Out!** activities challenge students to apply what they have learned.

**Sentence Structure, Grammar,** and **Mechanics** sections help students understand the building blocks of sentences and accurately construct different types of sentences.

## SENTENCE STRUCTURE

There are four basic sentence structures in English: (1) simple, (2) compound, (3) complex, and (4) compound-complex. In this chapter, you will learn about simple sentences.

### SIMPLE SENTENCES

A **simple sentence** is a sentence that has one subject-verb pair.

The subject (S) in a simple sentence may be a single subject (consisting of a word, noun phrase, or subject pronoun) or it may be **compound**. That is, it may consist of two or more subjects (nouns, noun phrases, or pronouns) joined by connecting words like *and* or *or*:

My brother (S) and I (S) are completely different.

Mary (S) or Rita (S) will meet you at the airport.

The verb (V) in a simple sentence may also be compound. It may consist of two or more verb forms joined by connecting words such as *and* or *or*. However, these are simple sentences because they have only one subject-verb pair.

They laughed (V) and cried (V) at the same time.

He walks (V) or cycles (V) to work.

Study the simple sentences in the left column and their patterns in the right column. There are many variations, but each sentence has only one S V pair.

| Simple Sentences | Patterns |
|---|---|
| 1. My younger sister (S) speaks (V) English well. | S V |
| 2. My mother (S) and father (S) speak (V) English well. | SS V |
| 3. My mother (S) and father (S) speak (V) and write (V) English well. | SS VV |
| 4. My brother (S) doesn't speak (V) or write (V) English well. | S VV |

20 CHAPTER 1

**Simple charts with clear examples** make the rules easy to see and remember.

| Capitalize the First Letter of | Examples | |
|---|---|---|
| 5. names of languages or nationalities that are the name or part of the name of a school subject | English<br>English history | Russian<br>Russian art |
| AND<br>names of school courses with numbers | English History 201 | Physics 352 |
| 6. specific places you can find on a map | England<br>First Street<br>New York City | South America<br>the Amazon River<br>Times Square |

**PRACTICE 7** **Editing Capitalization Errors**

Work alone or with a partner. Read the paragraph. Change the small letters to capital letters where needed.

M Z
mark zuckerberg

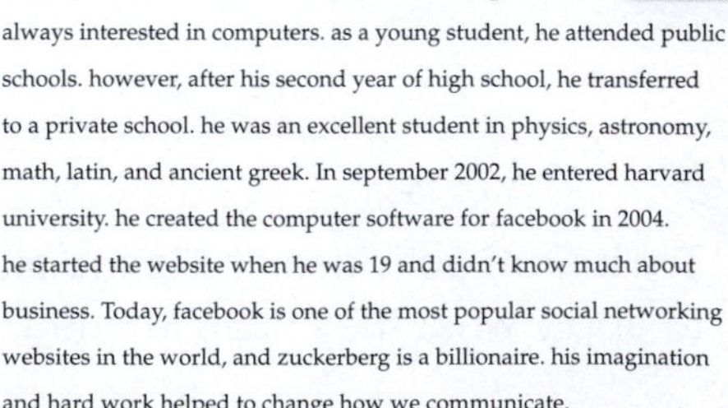

One of the most famous young entrepreneurs[1] in the united states is mark zuckerberg. he is the creator of a company called Facebook. zuckerberg was born in 1984 and grew up in dobbs ferry, new york. his father was a dentist, and his mother was a doctor. Zuckerberg was always interested in computers. as a young student, he attended public schools. however, after his second year of high school, he transferred to a private school. he was an excellent student in physics, astronomy, math, latin, and ancient greek. In september 2002, he entered harvard university. he created the computer software for facebook in 2004. he started the website when he was 19 and didn't know much about business. Today, facebook is one of the most popular social networking websites in the world, and zuckerberg is a billionaire. his imagination and hard work helped to change how we communicate.

[1] **entrepreneurs:** people who start companies, arrange business deals, and take risks in order to make a profit

Describing People 19

**Editing skills** are sharpened as students find and correct errors in sentences and paragraphs.

**Step-by-step Writing Assignments** make the writing process clear and easy to follow.

## WRITING ASSIGNMENT

Your writing assignment for this chapter is to write a paragraph about your family or about one person in your family. Use the writing models on pages 5 and 6 and the final draft of "My Grandmother" to help you. To complete the assignment, you will follow the steps in the writing process:

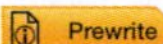

**STEP 1: Prewrite to get ideas.**

- Make a list of questions and then use the questions to interview one or more family members. Take notes during the interview.
- Review your notes and think about your topic.
- Freewrite about your topic for about ten minutes.
- Reread your freewriting and mark it up. Circle ideas that you will use in your paragraph. Cross out ideas that you won't use.
- Review the words in Looking at Vocabulary and Applying Vocabulary on pages 6–7 and 26. Look at your freewriting again and, if possible, add in some of these words.

**STEP 2: Write the first draft.**

- Write *FIRST DRAFT* at the top of your paper.
- Write the paragraph. Begin with a topic sentence that generally describes your family or family member.

  My family is small and close.

  My grandfather is old in years but young in spirit.

  My brother is the irresponsible one in our family.
- Write about eight to ten more supporting sentences about your family or family member. In these sentences, explain what you wrote in your first sentence. How does your family show that it is close? How does your grandfather show that he is young in spirit? In what ways is your brother irresponsible? Give examples.
- End your paragraph with a concluding sentence that relates back to your topic sentence and tells how you feel about your family or family member.

  Now we live far from each other, but we will always feel close in our hearts.

  My grandfather will always seem young to me.

  My brother will never grow up.

Describing People 31

**Peer Review** and **Writer's Self-Check Worksheets** at the back of the book help students collaborate and sharpen their revision skills.

**STEP 3: Revise and edit the draft.**

- Exchange papers with a partner and give each other feedback on your paragraphs. Use Chapter 1 Peer Review on page 206.
- Consider your partner's feedback and revise and edit your paragraph. Mark changes on your first draft.
- Check your paragraph carefully against Chapter 1 Writer's Self-Check on page 207, and make more changes as needed.

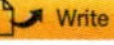

**STEP 4: Write a new draft.**

- Refer to the changes you made on your first draft and write a neat final copy of your paragraph.
- Proofread it carefully.
- Hand it in to your teacher. Your teacher may also ask you to hand in your prewriting and your first draft.

### SELF-ASSESSMENT

In this chapter, you learned to:

- ❍ Use questions and note taking to get ideas for writing
- ❍ Identify the three parts of a paragraph
- ❍ Use correct paragraph format
- ❍ Recognize subjects, verbs, and objects in complete sentences
- ❍ Use six rules of capitalization
- ❍ Work with simple sentences
- ❍ Write, revise, and edit a paragraph describing a person

Which ones can you do well? Mark them ✓

Which ones do you need to practice more? Mark them ✗

32 CHAPTER 1

NEW!

**Self-Assessment** encourages students to evaluate their progress.

NEW!

**Expansion sections** challenge students to build on the writing skills they have practiced in each chapter.

EXPANSION

### TIMED WRITING

To succeed in academic writing you need to be able to write quickly and fluently. For example, you might have to write a paragraph for a test in class, and you only have 30 minutes. In this activity, you will write a paragraph in class. You will have 30 minutes. To complete the activity in time, follow the directions.

1. Read the writing prompt below (or the prompt your teacher assigns) carefully. Make sure you understand the question or task. Then decide on the topic of your paragraph. (3 minutes)
2. Use clustering to get ideas. Decide which ideas you will write about and then make an outline to organize your ideas. (5 minutes)
3. Write your paragraph. Be sure to include a title, a topic sentence, listing-order transition signals, supporting ideas, and a concluding sentence. (15 minutes)
4. Proofread your paragraph. Correct any mistakes. (7 minutes)
5. Give your paper to your teacher.

**Prompt:** Write a listing-order paragraph about a teacher or a boss. What characteristics and abilities made the person memorable? Include examples to support your main ideas.

### YOUR JOURNAL

Continue making entries in your journal. If you cannot think of a topic for a journal entry, try one of these ideas:

- What career or profession are you interested in? Discuss two or three reasons for your interest. Support each reason with examples or explanations.
- Overall, was your high school experience positive or negative? Include three main reasons and support each one with examples or explanations.
- What are the most important characteristics for a friend to have? Write about two or three characteristics and say why they are important.

*For more ideas for journal entries, see Appendix A on page 193.*

Listing-Order Paragraphs 69

NEW!

**Timed Writing activities** help prepare students to write well on tests.

**Your Journal** encourages students to develop and increase written fluency.

# CHAPTER 1

# DESCRIBING PEOPLE

## OBJECTIVES

**Writers need certain skills.**

**In this chapter, you will learn to:**

- Use questions and note taking to get ideas for writing
- Identify the three parts of a paragraph
- Use correct paragraph format
- Recognize subjects, verbs, and objects in complete sentences
- Use six rules of capitalization
- Work with simple sentences
- Write, revise, and edit a paragraph describing a person

*Each person in a family is unique. Can you think of a different word to describe each person in this family?*

## INTRODUCTION

Academic writing is the kind of writing you do in high school and college. Its purpose is to explain something or to give information about something. Academic writing requires a number of skills. For example, you must be able to express an idea by arranging words in a correctly formed sentence (**sentence structure**). You must also be able to arrange your ideas in a well-organized paragraph (**organization**). And, of course, you must be able to write using correct **grammar** and **punctuation**.

In this chapter, you will learn how to write a well-organized paragraph about a person. You will learn about the parts of a paragraph and correct paragraph format. Then you will learn about the parts of a sentence and the structure of simple sentences.

To help you get ideas for writing, you will first do some prewriting.

## PREWRITING

Before you write, you need ideas to help you get started. In academic writing, it is often useful to write down your ideas so that you can begin to organize them into paragraphs. This is known as **prewriting**.

There are many different prewriting techniques. In this chapter, you will use two techniques: asking questions and taking notes. You will use these techniques to get ideas for a paragraph about one of your classmates. Later in the chapter, you will look at another prewriting technique known as freewriting (see page 27).

### ASKING QUESTIONS AND TAKING NOTES

Asking questions and taking notes are prewriting techniques that help you gather information and get ideas. When you take notes, you do not have to write complete sentences. Just write down the important information.

**PRACTICE 1** Interviewing a Classmate

**A** Look at the topics. Which topics are OK to ask about? Check (✓) *Yes* or *No.* Then add two more topics that you can ask about.

| Topics | OK to ask about? | |
|---|---|---|
| | Yes | No |
| 1. First and last name | ☑ | ☐ |
| 2. Age | ☐ | ☑ |
| 3. City and country | ☑ | ☐ |
| 4. Family status (married, single) | ☐ | ☐ |
| 5. Religion | ☐ | ☐ |
| 6. Address in this country | ☐ | ☐ |
| 7. Length of time in this country | ☐ | ☐ |
| 8. Length of time studying English | ☐ | ☐ |
| 9. Reasons for studying English | ☐ | ☐ |
| 10. Job or occupation | ☐ | ☐ |
| 11. Salary | ☐ | ☐ |
| 12. Hobbies or sports | ☐ | ☐ |
| 13. Weekend activities | ☐ | ☐ |
| 14. Plans for the future | ☐ | ☐ |
| 15. ____________________ | ☑ | ☐ |
| 16. ____________________ | ☑ | ☐ |

**B** On a separate sheet of paper, write a question for each *Yes* topic in Part A. Then compare questions with a partner. Make sure your question forms are correct.

*1. What is your name?*

*3. Where are you from?*

**C** Use your questions from Part B to interview a classmate. Take notes. Ask more questions to clarify spelling and other information. You will use this information in the Try It Out! activity on page 13.

| | |
|---|---|
| *What is your name?* | *Santy Valverde* |
| *Where are you from?* | *Michoacán, Mexico* |

## ORGANIZATION

A **paragraph** is a group of related sentences about a single topic. The topic of a paragraph contains one, and only one, idea. A paragraph has three main parts and they appear in this order:

- The **topic sentence** names the topic and tells what the paragraph will say about it. This sentence is usually the first sentence in a paragraph.
- The middle sentences in a paragraph are called the **supporting sentences** or **the body**. Supporting sentences give examples or other details about the topic. In some cases, they might even tell a story to illustrate the topic sentence.
- The last sentence in a paragraph is usually the **concluding sentence**. The concluding sentence often restates the topic sentence in different words or summarizes the main points.

A paragraph is like a sandwich: two pieces of bread (the topic and concluding sentences) holding the key ingredients (the supporting sentences).

## LOOKING AT THE MODELS

The writing models describe two people. Writing Model 1 is about a teacher, and Writing Model 2 is about someone's best friend.

**Work with a partner or in a small group. Read the models. Then answer the questions.**

### Writing Model 1

#### Mrs. Robinson

Mrs. Robinson, my first grade teacher, was an important person in my life. I was only six years old, but she taught me a valuable life lesson. In the schools in my country, children usually learn to print before they learn to write in cursive script (like handwriting). Mrs. Robinson didn't believe in printing. She thought it was a waste of time. She taught us to write in cursive script from the first day. At first it was hard, and she made us practice a lot. That made me angry because I wasn't very good at it. I remember filling entire pages just with capital Os. I didn't think I could ever learn to write beautifully, but Mrs. Robinson was patient with me and told me to keep trying. At the end of the year, I felt very grown up because I could write in cursive script. I was proud of my new skill. Mrs. Robinson was important to me because she taught me the value of hard work.

### Questions about the Model

1. Which sentence gives more information: the topic sentence or the concluding sentence?
2. How many supporting sentences does the paragraph have? How do they support the topic sentence: Do they give examples, or do they tell a story?

## Writing Model 2

### My Best Friend

My best friend, Freddie, has three important qualities. First of all, Freddie is always ready to have a good time, so I love spending time with him. Sometimes we play Frisbee in the park. He's very funny when he chases the Frisbee. Sometimes we just sit around in my room, listening to music and talking. Well, I talk, and he just listens. Second, Freddie is completely trustworthy. I can tell him my deepest secrets, and he doesn't share them with anyone else. Third, Freddie is caring and understands my moods. When I am tense, he tries to make me relax. When I am sad, he tries to comfort me. When I am happy, he is happy, too. To sum up, my best friend is fun to be with, trustworthy, and understanding—even if he is just a dog.

### Questions about the Model

1. Which sentence is longer: the topic sentence or the concluding sentence? Which of these two sentences has surprising information?
2. How many supporting sentences does the paragraph have? How do they support the topic sentence: Do they give examples, or do they tell a story?

## Looking at Vocabulary: Descriptive Adjectives

When you write about people, you need to use words that describe a person's personality and feelings. Learning synonyms[1] for common adjectives is a good way to expand your vocabulary and improve your writing.

Synonyms are especially helpful when you want to write more than one sentence about a particular part of someone's personality.

My teacher almost never gets **angry** with us. I've only seen her lose her temper once, and even then she didn't stay **mad** for more than a few seconds.

Rainy days make me feel **sad**. When the sun is out, I never feel **unhappy**.

[1] **synonym:** a word with the same or nearly the same meaning as another word

## PRACTICE 2 Looking at Descriptive Words

**A** Look at the adjectives in the first column of the chart. Find and circle them in Writing Models 1 and 2. The adjectives are in the order that they appear in the models.

| Descriptive Words | |
|---|---|
| **Adjectives** | **Synonyms** |
| angry | mad |
| patient | |
| grown up | |
| funny | |
| trustworthy | |
| caring | |
| tense | |
| sad | |

**B** Use the words from the box to complete the chart in Part A.

| | | | |
|---|---|---|---|
| amusing | dependable | ~~mad~~ | nervous |
| calm | kind | mature | unhappy |

**C** Use the words in Part B again to complete the sentences. Two of the words are extra.

1. Nadia isn't talking to her cousin Jamal. She's ____mad____ at him because he forgot her birthday.
2. Some students learn more slowly than others, so teachers need to be ________________.
3. Diego has a big job interview on Monday. He's very ________________ about it.
4. Rita's daughter is only 10 years old, but she seems older. She's very ________________ for her age.
5. I can tell my best friend anything, and I know she won't tell others. She's very ________________.
6. My sons are very ________________. They always make me laugh.

## FORMATTING THE PAGE

As you saw on page 4, a well-organized paragraph needs to have a topic sentence, supporting sentences, and a concluding sentence. In addition, it needs to use correct paragraph format. In this section, you will learn about correct paragraph format, and then you will use it in a short writing activity.

In academic writing, instructors require students to use correct format for paragraphs. Look at the guidelines and models for handwritten and computer-written work. Your instructor may have other requirements, so be sure to follow them.

### Page Format for Handwritten Work

#### The Paper

Use 8½-inch-by-11-inch lined paper with three holes. The holes should be on your left side as you write. Write on one side of the paper only.

#### The Ink

Use black or dark blue ink only. Do not use pencil.

#### The Heading

Write your full name in the upper left corner in the wide, unlined area at the top of the page. Under it, write the course name and number. Below that, write the date the assignment is due in the order month-day-year, with a comma after the day.

#### The Title

Center the title of your paragraph on the first line.

#### The Paragraph

Skip one line, and start your paragraph on the third line. Remember to indent the first word about ½ inch from the left margin. (*Indent* means to leave some space at the beginning of the line.)

#### Margins

Leave a 1-inch margin on the left and right sides of the paper. Also leave a 1-inch margin at the bottom of the page. Your teacher may use these empty spaces to write comments to you.

#### Spacing

Leave a blank line between each line of writing. You and your teacher can use this space for corrections, comments, and revisions.

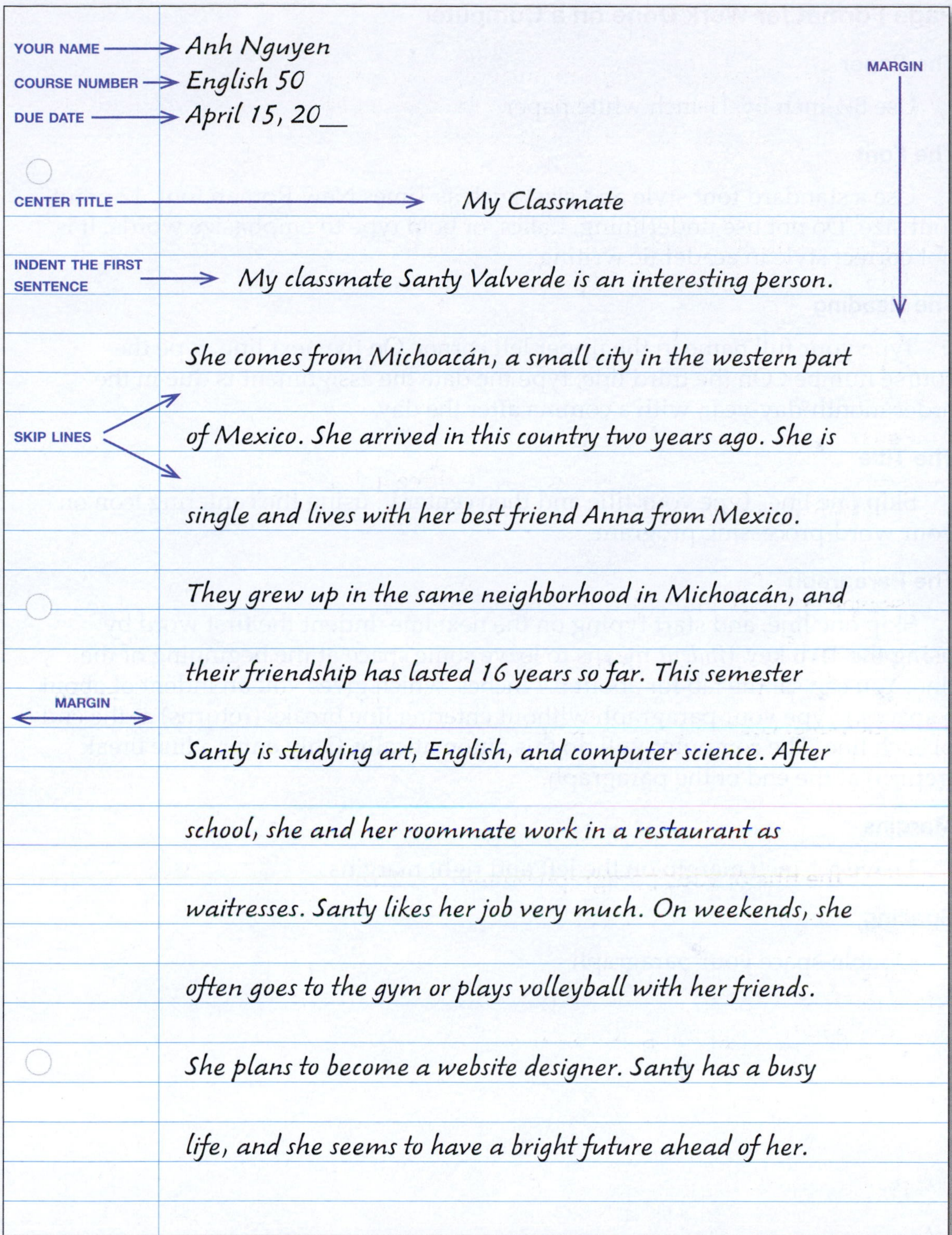

YOUR NAME
Anh Nguyen
COURSE NUMBER
English 50
DUE DATE
April 15, 20__
MARGIN
CENTER TITLE
My Classmate
INDENT THE FIRST SENTENCE
My classmate Santy Valverde is an interesting person.
She comes from Michoacán, a small city in the western part
SKIP LINES
of Mexico. She arrived in this country two years ago. She is
single and lives with her best friend Anna from Mexico.
They grew up in the same neighborhood in Michoacán, and
their friendship has lasted 16 years so far. This semester
MARGIN
Santy is studying art, English, and computer science. After
school, she and her roommate work in a restaurant as
waitresses. Santy likes her job very much. On weekends, she
often goes to the gym or plays volleyball with her friends.
She plans to become a website designer. Santy has a busy
life, and she seems to have a bright future ahead of her.

## Page Format for Work Done on a Computer

### The Paper

Use 8½-inch-by-11-inch white paper.

### The Font

Use a standard font style and size, such as Times New Roman font, 12 point font size. Do not use underlining, italics, or bold type to emphasize words. It is not correct style in academic writing.

### The Heading

Type your full name in the upper left corner. On the next line, type the course number. On the third line, type the date the assignment is due in the order month-day-year, with a comma after the day.

### The Title

Skip one line. Type your title and then center it, using the centering icon on your word-processing program.

### The Paragraph

Skip one line, and start typing on the next line. Indent the first word by using the TAB key. (*Indent* means to leave some space at the beginning of the line. You can set the tab for about 0.4 inches, which gives you an indent of about 5 spaces.) Type your paragraph without entering line breaks (returns) at the end of each line. The computer will do this automatically. Only enter a line break (return) at the end of the paragraph.

### Margins

Leave a 1-inch margin on the left and right margins.

### Spacing

Double-space your paragraph.

YOUR NAME → Sacha Petrovsky

COURSE NUMBER → English 50

DUE DATE → April 15, 20__

CENTER TITLE → My Classmate

USE **TAB** KEY TO INDENT FIRST SENTENCE (ABOUT **5** SPACES) → Antonio Gonsalves is my classmate from Brazil. He is very athletic. His friends call him Tony. He is the oldest son in his family. He moved here four years ago to live with his aunt and uncle and to learn English. He plans to major in Business Administration and then return to Brazil to work in his family's hotel business. One interesting thing I learned about Tony is that he is a big sports fan. He watches sports on TV all the time and follows sports news online. He also plays several sports, but his favorite sport is soccer. After all, he is from Brazil. I like Tony's enthusiasm. I look forward to working together in class and maybe playing soccer after class.

MARGIN

DOUBLE SPACE

MARGIN

## Editing Paragraph Format

**Editing** is an important part of producing a well-organized paragraph. Editing means checking for mistakes and making corrections. When you edit, one of the things you should check for is mistakes in paragraph format.

### PRACTICE 3 Editing Paragraph Format

Work alone or with a partner. Find the mistakes in the format of the paragraph. Then rewrite the paragraph on a separate sheet of paper using correct format. Remember to skip lines when you rewrite the paragraph.

English 10-A Amy Wong
Sept 5

My Classmate

My classmate is a very nice person. Her name is
Phuong Pham.
She is from Vietnam. In Vietnam she was a pharmacist.

She is married.
She lives with her husband, her children, and her
husband's parents in a house. Phuong is taking two English
courses, one health science course, and one math course.
She likes to listen to
music and to read books.
She doesn't have a job right now, but she plans to
get one when she finishes school. I enjoyed meeting
Phuong Pham.

**TRY IT OUT!** **On a separate sheet of paper, write a paragraph about the classmate you interviewed in Practice 1 on pages 3–4. Follow these directions.**

1. Give your paragraph a title, such as "My Classmate" or "My New Classmate."
2. Begin with a topic sentence that tells your classmate's name and generally describes his or her personality. You can use a word from the chart in Practice 2 on page 7, a word from the word box, or your own idea.

| | | | |
|---|---|---|---|
| **cheerful** | **fun-loving** | **likeable** | **serious** |
| **energetic** | **hard-working** | **outgoing** | **soft-spoken** |
| **friendly** | **interesting** | **quiet** | **talented** |

*My classmate Rolanda Martin is an interesting young woman.*

*My new classmate Franco Alvarez is a friendly person.*

3. Write supporting sentences about your classmate. Use your notes from your interview in Practice 1 on pages 3–4 to give you ideas.
4. End your paragraph with a concluding sentence that tells how you feel about your classmate.

*I look forward to sharing ideas and interests with Rolanda.*

*I am happy to have Franco as my classmate.*

5. Check your paragraph format. Is it correct? (See pages 8–11.)
6. Proofread your paragraph, and correct any mistakes.

**Writing Tip**

Your topic sentence should be a general statement about your classmate's personality. It should not have specific facts about your classmate. Your supporting sentences will have the specific facts.

APPROPRIATE: My classmate Ana Wong is an energetic young woman. *(general)*

NOT APPROPRIATE: My classmate is from China. *(too specific)*
My classmate is married. *(too specific)*

## GRAMMAR AND MECHANICS

In Organization on page 4, you learned that a paragraph is a group of related sentences about a single topic. Now you will look more closely at sentences.

### SENTENCES

A **sentence** is a group of words that contains a subject and a verb and expresses a complete thought. A sentence begins with a capital letter and ends with a period or question mark. A sentence may also end with an exclamation point, but in academic writing, most sentences end with a period.

SUBJECT VERB
He is a graduate student.

It is hot today.

He looks mad.

Are you ready?

Who's there?

Here are some common errors that students make when writing sentences:

- **There is no subject.** In some languages, you can leave out a subject pronoun (*he*, *she*, *it*, *we*, *you*, and *they*) when the meaning is clear without it. Sentences in English require a subject. (Commands are an exception. See page 18.)

  INCORRECT: Is very trustworthy.

  CORRECT: He is very trustworthy.

- **There is no verb.** In some languages, you can leave out a verb like *is* or *are* when the meaning is clear without it. Sentences in English require a verb.

  INCORRECT: The instructor strict.

  CORRECT: The instructor is intelligent.

- **The thought is not complete.** A group of words that begins with a word such as *when*, *if*, or *because* and is followed by a subject and verb is not a complete thought. To be complete, the sentence must have another group of words with another subject and verb. (You will learn more about sentences like this in Chapter 3.)

  INCORRECT: **When** I finish my education.

  CORRECT: **When** I finish my education**,** I will work for my uncle.

## PRACTICE 4 Recognizing Sentences

**A** **Work with a partner. Read each group of words and write *S* (sentence) or *NS* (not a sentence).**

_____ 1. Is very hot today.

_____ 2. It is very hot today.

_____ 3. My new classmate from Brazil.

_____ 4. He speaks three languages fluently.

_____ 5. Is very competitive.

_____ 6. Hurry up, please.

_____ 7. He wants to start his own business.

_____ 8. He isn't married.

_____ 9. Enjoys music, especially jazz.

_____ 10. Don't send text messages in class.

_____ 11. The books expensive.

_____ 12. Go to the course website.

**B** **Correct the sentences that you marked with *NS* in Part A. Use the editing symbol "^" to insert the missing words.**

_____ 1. Is very hot today.

### Subjects, Verbs, and Objects

As you have already seen on page 14, sentences in English need to have a subject and a verb. Some sentences also need objects. In this section, you will learn how to recognize these three parts of a sentence. This will help you edit your writing.

- The **subject** tells who or what the sentence is about. It can be a noun (*Diego, college, students*), a noun phrase[1], or a subject pronoun (*I, you, he, she, it, we,* or *they*).

  Mark lost his keys.
  *(Who lost his keys?—Mark)*

  The cat chased the mouse.
  *(What chased the mouse?—the cat)*

  Soccer and tennis are my favorite sports.
  *(What are my favorite sports?—soccer and tennis)*

[1] **noun phrase:** a group of words ending with a noun that belong together in meaning (*my friends, a black dog, her husband's two cousins, Miguel and Maria*)

There are two kinds of **verbs**: action verbs and linking verbs.

- **Action verbs** name an action, such as *lose*, *chase*, *live*, *speak*, *go*, and *come*.

  Mark lost his keys.

  The cat chased the mouse.

  My family lives in a two-bedroom apartment.

- **Linking verbs** do not express an action. Instead, they connect the subject of the sentence to information about the subject. For example, a linking verb can connect the subject to another noun that tells you who or what the subject is, or to an adjective that describes the subject. The most common linking verbs are *be, become, look, feel, seem, smell, sound,* and *taste*.

  Soccer and tennis are my favorite sports.

  I feel lucky today.

  The air smells fresh and clean.

Some sentences (but not all) have an object. The **object** receives the action of certain action verbs. It can be a noun (*Diego, college, students*), a noun phrase, an object pronoun (*me, you, him, her, it, us,* or *them)* or a possessive pronoun (*mine, yours, his, hers, ours, theirs*). To find an object, make a question by putting *who(m)* or *what* after an action verb.

Mark lost **his keys**.
*(Lost what?—his keys.* His keys *is an object.)*

His girlfriend found **them**.
*(Found what?—them.* Them *is an object.)*

The cat chased **the mouse**.
*(chased who[m] or what?—the mouse.* The mouse *is an object.)*

**Writing Tip**

Certain verbs (called *transitive verbs*) must have objects. Some of these are *buy*, *give*, *have*, *like*, *love*, *need*, *own*, *place*, *put*, *spend*, and *want*.

They need some money.

I don't want it.

## PRACTICE 5 Identifying Subjects, Verbs, and Objects

**Look at each sentence. Underline the subject once and write *S* above it. Underline the verb twice, and write *V* above it. Circle the object (if there is one), and write *O* above it. Some sentences have more than one verb and object.**

1. My youngest brother is in high school.
2. He watches TV and does his homework at the same time.
3. He works at a department store.
4. He likes his job but doesn't like his boss.
5. His job is easy and pays well.
6. This semester, he is taking extra classes.
7. He became a computer programmer at the age of 16.
8. He speaks and understands English very well.
9. On weekends, he plays soccer with his friends.
10. He doesn't have a girlfriend yet.

## PRACTICE 6 Editing Subject and Verb Errors

**Work alone or with a partner. Find the seven missing subjects and verbs in the paragraph. Make corrections.**

### Larry's Bad Habit

My friend Larry a bad habit. He never on time to anything. Arrives ten minutes late everywhere. Larry always an excuse. "I missed the bus." "My alarm clock didn't ring." "My watch stopped." Uses each excuse at least twice a week. I know them all. Whenever Larry rushes in—ten minutes late, of course—and starts to say, "Sorry I'm late, but I . . . ," I can finish the sentence for him. However, I recently discovered a new strategy. If the movie starts at 7:00, I tell Larry it starts at 6:45. Then he early! Larry's bad habit not a problem for me any longer.

### Commands

Commands are sentences that look like they do not have subjects, but in fact they do. We may not write the subject or say it, but we understand that the subject is *you* (the person that the command is addressed to).

| COMMANDS | NEGATIVE COMMANDS |
|---|---|
| (~~You~~) Be quiet. | (~~You~~) Don't eat so much! |
| (~~You~~) Wait for me! | (~~You~~) Don't forget to call home. |
| (~~You~~) Speak slowly. | (~~You~~) Don't worry. |

## CAPITALIZATION

In English, there are many rules for using capital letters. Here are six important ones:

| CAPITALIZE THE FIRST LETTER OF | EXAMPLES |
|---|---|
| **1.** the first word in a sentence | My neighbor is a mechanic. |
| **2.** the pronoun *I* | My friends and I often study together. |
| **3.** names of people and their titles | King Abdullah II<br>President Lincoln<br>Professor Patrick Jones<br>Mr. and Mrs. Harold Simpson |
| NOTE: Do not capitalize a title without a name except when the reference is to a specific person who holds the title. | The President and the First Lady had dinner with the Queen and her husband last night. *(The titles refer to specific people.)*<br>COMPARE:<br>I've never met a king or a president.<br>He wants to be a math professor. *(The references are general, so you must not capitalize the titles.)* |
| **4.** nationalities, languages, religions, and ethnic groups | English, Spanish, Swedish, Latin, Mandarin, Farsi<br>Christian, Jewish, Muslim, Hispanic, Native American |

| Capitalize the First Letter of | Examples | |
|---|---|---|
| **5.** names of languages or nationalities that are the name or part of the name of a school subject | English<br>English history | Russian<br>Russian art |
| AND | | |
| names of school courses with numbers | English History 201 | Physics 352 |
| **6.** specific places you can find on a map | England<br>First Street<br>New York City | South America<br>the Amazon River<br>Times Square |

## PRACTICE 7 Editing Capitalization Errors

**Work alone or with a partner. Read the paragraph. Change the small letters to capital letters where needed.**

### mark zuckerberg

One of the most famous young entrepreneurs[1] in the united states is mark zuckerberg. he is the creator of a company called Facebook. zuckerberg was born in 1984 and grew up in dobbs ferry, new york. his father was a dentist, and his mother was a doctor. Zuckerberg was always interested in computers. as a young student, he attended public schools. however, after his second year of high school, he transferred to a private school. he was an excellent student in physics, astronomy, math, latin, and ancient greek. In september 2002, he entered harvard university. he created the computer software for facebook in 2004. he started the website when he was 19 and didn't know much about business. Today, facebook is one of the most popular social networking websites in the world, and zuckerberg is a billionaire. his imagination and hard work helped to change how we communicate.

[1] **entrepreneurs:** people who start companies, arrange business deals, and take risks in order to make a profit

## SENTENCE STRUCTURE

There are four basic sentence structures in English: (1) simple, (2) compound, (3) complex, and (4) compound-complex. In this chapter, you will learn about simple sentences.

### SIMPLE SENTENCES

A **simple sentence** is a sentence that has one subject-verb pair.

The subject (S) in a simple sentence may be a single subject (consisting of a word, noun phrase, or subject pronoun) or it may be **compound**. That is, it may consist of two or more subjects (nouns, noun phrases, or pronouns) joined by connecting words like *and* or *or*:

My brother (S) and I (S) are completely different.

Mary (S) or Rita (S) will meet you at the airport.

The verb (V) in a simple sentence may also be compound. It may consist of two or more verb forms joined by connecting words such as *and* or *or*. However, these are simple sentences because they have only one subject-verb pair.

They laughed (V) and cried (V) at the same time.

He walks (V) or cycles (V) to work.

Study the simple sentences in the left column and their patterns in the right column. There are many variations, but each sentence has only one S V pair.

| SIMPLE SENTENCES | PATTERNS |
|---|---|
| 1. My younger sister (S) speaks (V) English well. | S V |
| 2. My mother (S) and father (S) speak (V) English well. | SS V |
| 3. My mother (S) and father (S) speak (V) and write (V) English well. | SS VV |
| 4. My brother (S) doesn't speak (V) or write (V) English well. | S VV |

## Analyzing Your Writing for Verbs

Here are some simple rules to follow when you analyze your writing for verbs.

| RULES | EXAMPLES |
|---|---|
| **1.** Label two- and three-word verb forms as a single verb. | My sister is studying French this semester.<br>My brother has been living in Mexico since last year. |
| **2.** Label only main verb forms as verbs. Do not label infinitives (that is, verb forms which begin with *to*). | My grandmother wants to live in Florida.<br>Florida is a nice place to live |
| **3.** Do not label verb forms that are used as adjectives or nouns. | A duck is swimming in the hotel swimming pool. |

**PRACTICE 8** **Recognizing Patterns in Simple Sentences**

**A** Read the paragraph. Underline each subject once, and write *S* above it. Underline each verb twice, and write *V* above it.

### My Grandfather

1 My grandfather is old in years but young in spirit. 2 Every day, he swims a mile and works in his garden. 3 He and my grandmother have four children and ten grandchildren. 4 My grandfather loves parties and invites our entire family to his house for a big dinner on his birthday. 5 All 20 of us eat and tell stories half the night. 6 My grandfather never gets tired and is always the last to go to bed. 7 On his last birthday, my brothers and I gave him a present. 8 We put our money together and bought him a video game system. 9 Now he invites us to his house every weekend to play video games with him. 10 My grandfather never seems old to me.

**B** Write the pattern for each section in Part A.

1. S V
2. S VV
3. 
4. 
5. 
6. 
7. 
8. 
9. 
10. 

PRACTICE 9 **Using Simple Sentence Patterns**

**A** Write simple sentences about your family and friends. Use each of these patterns at least once: S V, SS V, S VV, and SS VV.

1. My youngest brother Jonathan goes to the University of Washington and works part time.
2. 
3. 
4. 
5. 
6. 

**B** Write the pattern for each sentence in Part A.

1. S VV
2. 
3. 
4. 
5. 
6. 

## Connecting Words: *And* and *Or*

You often need to connect words or groups of words in a sentence. One way to do this is to use a connecting word. Connecting words are called **conjunctions**. There are many conjunctions in English. Two of the most common ones are ***and*** and ***or***. They have different meanings.

| RULES | EXAMPLES |
|---|---|
| 1. *And* joins two or more similar things in affirmative sentences. | I like Chinese and Italian food.<br>We have class on Mondays, Wednesdays, and Fridays. |
| 2. *Or* connects two or more similar things in negative sentences. | I don't like warm milk or cold coffee.<br>We don't have class on Tuesdays or Thursdays. |
| 3. *Or* also connects two or more choices or alternatives. | I would like to go to London, Rome, or Paris on my next vacation.<br>(*I cannot go to all three places. I will choose one.*)<br>My father or my mother will meet me at the airport.<br>(*This sentence means that only one person will come to the airport.*)<br>COMPARE: My father and my mother will meet me at the airport. (*This sentence means that two people will come to the airport.*) |

**PRACTICE 10** **Using *And* and *Or***

Complete each sentence with *and* or *or*.

1. I can speak ___and___ understand English.
2. I can't speak Tagalog ___and or___ Vietnamese.
3. My mother is proud of my sister ___and___ me.
4. Would you like to listen to music ___or___ watch a movie? (*You can do only one.*)
5. You can walk there ___or___ take the bus. (*You can do only one.*)
6. My uncle, a talented artist, paints ___and___ makes sculptures.
7. Does your English class meet on Monday, Wednesday, ___and___ Friday, ___or___ on Tuesday, Thursday, ___and___ Friday?
8. Last year my stepmother graduated from college ___and___ started her own business.

# SENTENCE COMBINING

You can use the conjunctions *and* and *or* to combine short sentences into longer ones. When you do this, your writing is smoother and your ideas are easier to understand.

Here are four general principles to follow when you combine sentences:

- Whenever possible, don't repeat words.

  UNCOMBINED: I am a man. I am famous.

  COMBINED: **I am** a famous man.

- Add a connecting word like *and* when necessary.

  UNCOMBINED: She is attractive. She is intelligent.

  COMBINED: She is attractive **and** intelligent.

- Change words when necessary.

  UNCOMBINED: Blue is my favorite color. Yellow is my favorite color.

  COMBINED: Blue and yellow **are** my favorite color**s**.

- When you omit words, don't leave out words that provide important information.

  UNCOMBINED: He has short white hair. He has a long white beard.

  COMBINED: He has short white hair **and** a long white beard.

  You have to repeat the word *white* when you combine the sentences in the last example because it provides information about the man's hair and beard. If you leave it out of one or both parts of the sentence, the meaning changes.

**PRACTICE 11** **Combining Sentences with *And* and *Or***

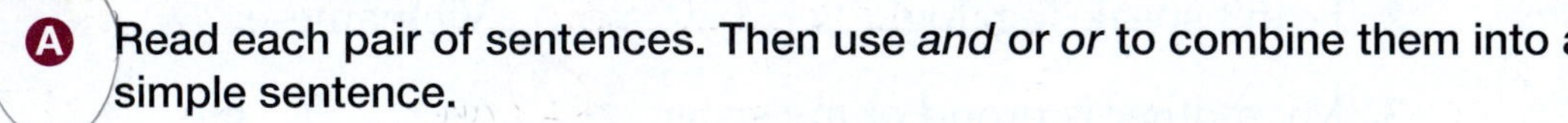

**A** Read each pair of sentences. Then use *and* or *or* to combine them into a simple sentence.

1. My brother speaks German. My brother speaks Japanese.

   My brother speaks German and Japanese.

2. Marie got an A in Biology 101. Marie got a B in English 103.

   Marie got an A in Biology and a B in English 103.

3. You can fly from Paris to Amsterdam. You can take a train from Paris to Amsterdam. *(You can't do both.)*

You can fly or take a train from Paris to Amsterdam.

4. Marta is married. Marta has two children.

Marta is married and has two children

5. She may major in math. She may major in business. (*She can't major in both.)*

She may major in math or business.

6. Should we go out tonight? Should we stay home tonight?

Should we go out or stay home tonight?

**B** **Combine each pair of sentences. There may be more than one answer.**

**Who Am I?**

1. I am a popular student on campus. I am a famous animal on campus at the University of California, Los Angeles.

I am a popular student and a famous animal on campus at the University of California, Los Angeles.

2. At every basketball game, I wear a costume. It's a bear costume.

At every basketball game, I wear a bear costume.

3. I have big brown ears. I have a black nose.

I have big brown ears and a black nose.

4. Over the costume, I always wear blue shorts. I always wear a white shirt.

Over the costume, I always wear blue shorts and a white shirt.

5. I look like a bear at the games. I act like a bear at the games.

I look ~~or~~ and act like a bear at the games

*(continued on next page)*

6. During the games, the cheerleaders are very enthusiastic. I am very enthusiastic.

During the games., the cheerleaders and I am very enthusiastic

7. We cheer for the UCLA team. We jump up and down.

We cheer for the UCLA from and we jump up and down

We cheer and jump up and down for the UCLA team

8. I sometimes hug a player. I sometimes joke with a referee. (*I don't do these things at the same time*).

I sometimes hug a player or joke with a referee.

9. I act funny. I make people laugh.

I act funny and make people laugh.

10. I am the team mascot[1]. The team is the UCLA basketball team.

I am the UCLA basketball team is mascot.

## Applying Vocabulary: Using Descriptive Adjectives

Before you begin your writing assignment, review what you learned about adjectives that describe personalities and feelings on pages 6–7.

**PRACTICE 12** **Using Synonyms**

**Use the synonym pairs in the box to write two related sentences about the people listed.**

| | |
|---|---|
| **angry – mad** | **patient – calm** |
| **caring – kind** | **sad – unhappy** |
| **funny – amusing** | **tense – nervous** |
| **grown up – mature** | **trustworthy – dependable** |

1. A classmate: *Hiro looks unhappy today. He says rainy days always make him feel sad.*

2. A family member: ______________________________

3. A good friend: ______________________________

[1] **mascot:** an animal that represents a team and brings good luck

4. A teacher: ______________________________________________

______________________________________________

5. Yourself: ______________________________________________

______________________________________________

## THE WRITING PROCESS

Good writing is more than just sitting down and "talking" on a piece of paper. It involves thinking, planning, writing, and revising. You become a good writer by always using these four steps:

1. Prewrite to get ideas.
2. Write the first draft.
3. Revise and edit the first draft.
4. Write a new draft.

### STEP 1: Prewrite to get ideas.

In the prewriting step, you get ideas to write about. Taking notes is one way to get ideas. You did this kind of prewriting for the paragraph you wrote about a classmate. Another way to get ideas is **freewriting**.

To freewrite, choose a topic and write it at the top of a piece of paper. Then write whatever sentences and words come into your mind about the topic. Write horizontally across the paper as you do when you write a letter.

Don't worry about grammar, spelling, or punctuation, and don't worry about putting your ideas into any kind of order. You don't even have to write complete sentences. Just write everything that comes into your mind about your topic. If you can't think of an English word, write it in your own language. The goal is to keep writing without stopping for about ten minutes or until you run out of ideas.

After you have run out of ideas, reread your freewriting. Choose one main idea for your paragraph. Then cross out ideas that aren't related to the one main idea.

Look at the examples of freewriting on the next page.

In this freewriting, the writer began by writing her topic at the top of the page. She then wrote whatever words and phrases came into her mind. Note that she will correct her mistakes in a later draft.

Freewriting about My Grandmother

My grandmother. She was a good cook. The best cook. Every weekend we have a big dinner. With big, big bowls of food. Lots of talking. Everybody in the family there. Every time we eat the same food, but we always love it. Is our favorite meal. She never mad at us. She always defends us when we are in trouble with our parents. One time I picked all the roses in her garden. She not even mad then. Grandmother kind and generous. She gives food to poor people. She never makes them feel bad about taking it. Makes people feel good, just as she made me feel good when I picked all the roses. Thanked me for the beautiful bouquet. Mother really angry. Grandmother always forgives. Forgiving heart.

When the writer reread her freewriting, she decided to focus on her grandmother's kindness and forgiving heart. She then crossed out the parts about cooking and food. Here is what her edited freewriting looks like:

Freewriting about My Grandmother

My grandmother. ~~She was a good cook. The best cook. Every weekend we have a big dinner. With big, big bowls of food. Lots of talking. Everybody in the family there. Every time we eat the same food, but we always love it. Is our favorite meal.~~ She never mad at us. She always defends us when we are in trouble with our parents. One time I picked all the roses in her garden. She not even mad then. Grandmother kind and generous. She gives food to poor people. She never makes them feel bad about taking it. Makes people feel good, just as she made me feel good when I picked all the roses. Thanked me for the beautiful bouquet. Mother really angry. Grandmother always forgives. Forgiving heart.

## STEP 2: Write the first draft.

In the second step, you write your paragraph in rough form without worrying too much about errors. This first writing is called the **first draft** or the **rough draft**.

Here is what the writer's computer-written first draft looks like:

> My Grandmother
>
> My grandmother kind and generous. She never mad at us. She always makes people feel good. One time I picked all the roses in her garden. She not even mad then. She made me feel good. Thanked me for the beautiful bouquet. Grandmother gives food to poor people. She never makes them feel bad about taking it. Makes people feel good, just as she made me feel good when I picked all the roses. Grandmother always forgive. Forgiving heart.

## STEP 3: Revise and edit the draft.

In the third step, you revise and edit your paragraph. When you revise, you make changes to make your ideas clearer and better organized. When you edit, you check and correct the language, grammar, punctuation, format, and spelling. Sometimes you might want to ask a classmate (a "peer") to read your work and make suggestions about how to improve your writing. This is called a "peer review." This feedback is often useful for showing you which parts of your paragraph you could improve. You will get a chance to see how this works when you do the Writing Assignment on pages 31–32.

When the writer of the example revised and edited her first draft, she made her corrections directly on the first draft. These are the types of corrections she made:

- She crossed out unnecessary sentences.
- She added missing subjects and verbs.
- She changed the concluding sentence to make it more like the topic sentence.

You can see her revisions and edits on the next page.

Here is what her marked-up draft looks like:

My Grandmother

is

My grandmother ^ kind and generous. ~~She never mad at us.~~

She always makes people feel good. One time I picked all the

wasn't

roses in her garden. She ^ ~~not~~ even mad then. ~~She made me feel~~

She thanked also

~~good. Thanked~~ ^ me for the beautiful bouquet. Grandmother ^

gives food to poor people. She never makes them feel bad about

She makes them

taking it. ^ ~~Makes people~~ feel good, just as she made me feel

I will always remember my grandmother's

good when I picked all the roses. ^ ~~Grandmother always forgive.~~

kindness and generosity.

~~Forgiving heart~~.

## STEP 4: Write a new draft.

In the last step, you look at the revisions and edits you made to your first draft in Step 3 and you make a clean copy of your paragraph to hand in to your teacher. Here is what the writer's final draft looks like:

My Grandmother

My grandmother is kind and generous. She always makes people feel good. One time I picked all the roses in her garden. She wasn't even mad then. She thanked me for the beautiful bouquet. Grandmother also gives food to poor people. She never makes them feel bad about taking it. She makes them feel good, just as she made me feel good when I picked all the roses. I will always remember my grandmother's kindness and generosity.

## WRITING ASSIGNMENT

Your writing assignment for this chapter is to write a paragraph about your family or about one person in your family. Use the writing models on pages 5 and 6 and the final draft of "My Grandmother" to help you. To complete the assignment, you will follow the steps in the writing process:

### STEP 1: Prewrite to get ideas.

- Make a list of questions and then use the questions to interview one or more family members. Take notes during the interview.
- Review your notes and think about your topic.
- Freewrite about your topic for about ten minutes.
- Reread your freewriting and mark it up. Circle ideas that you will use in your paragraph. Cross out ideas that you won't use.
- Review the words in Looking at Vocabulary and Applying Vocabulary on pages 6–7 and 26. Look at your freewriting again and, if possible, add in some of these words.

### STEP 2: Write the first draft.

- Write *FIRST DRAFT* at the top of your paper.
- Write the paragraph. Begin with a topic sentence that generally describes your family or family member.

  My family is small and close.

  My grandfather is old in years but young in spirit.

  My brother is the irresponsible one in our family.

- Write about eight to ten more supporting sentences about your family or family member. In these sentences, explain what you wrote in your first sentence. How does your family show that it is close? How does your grandfather show that he is young in spirit? In what ways is your brother irresponsible? Give examples.
- End your paragraph with a concluding sentence that relates back to your topic sentence and tells how you feel about your family or family member.

  Now we live far from each other, but we will always feel close in our hearts.

  My grandfather will always seem young to me.

  My brother will never grow up.

### STEP 3: Revise and edit the draft.

- Exchange papers with a partner and give each other feedback on your paragraphs. Use Chapter 1 Peer Review on page 206.
- Consider your partner's feedback and revise and edit your paragraph. Mark changes on your first draft.
- Check your paragraph carefully against Chapter 1 Writer's Self-Check on page 207, and make more changes as needed.

### STEP 4: Write a new draft.

- Refer to the changes you made on your first draft and write a neat final copy of your paragraph.
- Proofread it carefully.
- Hand it in to your teacher. Your teacher may also ask you to hand in your prewriting and your first draft.

## SELF-ASSESSMENT

**In this chapter, you learned to:**

- ❍ Use questions and note taking to get ideas for writing
- ❍ Identify the three parts of a paragraph
- ❍ Use correct paragraph format
- ❍ Recognize subjects, verbs, and objects in complete sentences
- ❍ Use six rules of capitalization
- ❍ Work with simple sentences
- ❍ Write, revise, and edit a paragraph describing a person

**Which ones can you do well? Mark them ✓**

**Which ones do you need to practice more? Mark them ✗**

# EXPANSION

## TIMED WRITING

To succeed in academic writing you need to be able to write quickly and fluently. For example, you might have to write a paragraph for a test in class, and you only have 30 minutes. In this activity, you will write a paragraph in class. You will have 30 minutes. To complete the activity in time, follow the directions.

1. Read the writing prompt below (or the prompt your teacher assigns) carefully.
2. Make sure you understand the question or task. Then decide on the topic of your paragraph. (3 minutes)
3. Write some notes to get ideas and list some describing words. Decide which ideas you will write about. (5 minutes)
4. Write your paragraph. Be sure to include a title, a topic sentence, supporting ideas, and a concluding sentence. (15 minutes)
5. Proofread your paragraph. Correct any mistakes. (7 minutes)
6. Give your paper to your teacher.

**Prompt:** Write a paragraph about a person you admire. You can write about someone you know (a friend or a family member) or about a famous person. Describe his or her personality. Include supporting sentences with examples that show you admire this person. (30 minutes)

## YOUR JOURNAL

When you keep a journal, you write about your life and your thoughts. Journal writing allows you to practice new skills without worrying about a grade. It also gives you a chance to practice using new vocabulary, and it will help you improve your writing fluency and skills.

Your teacher may ask you to write for a certain amount of time every day or every week, or he or she may ask you to write a certain number of pages. It is a good idea to write the date and your starting and stopping times above each entry. For your journal writing, your teacher may assign a topic to you or allow you to write about anything you choose. He or she may also ask you to write about one of the topics provided at the end of Chapters 2–6.

Here is a suggested topic for your first journal entry:

- Introduce yourself to your teacher. Write about your childhood, your hometown, your family, your education, your hobbies, or anything else that you think your teacher might find interesting.

Remember to leave space in the margins for your teacher to make comments or ask for more information.

*For more ideas for journal entries, see Appendix A on page 193.*

# CHAPTER 2 LISTING-ORDER PARAGRAPHS

## OBJECTIVES

**Writers need certain skills.**

**In this chapter, you will learn to:**

- Use clustering to get ideas for writing
- Identify the three parts of a listing-order paragraph
- Use listing-order transition signals and conclusion signals
- Organize ideas with an outline
- Work with compound sentences
- Identify and correct run-ons and comma splices
- Use listing order to write a paragraph related to a career

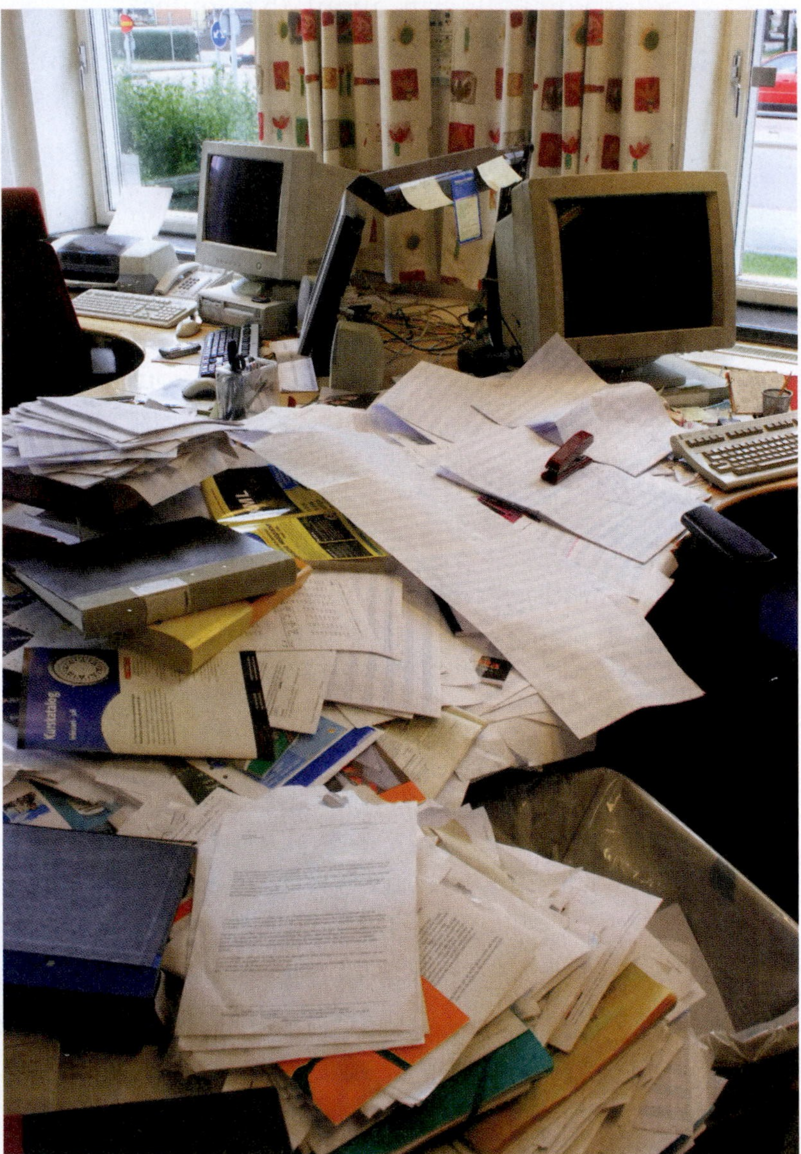

*A messy, disorganized desk can hurt productivity. Can you think of three improvements the person who works here might make to create a better, more organized workspace?*

## INTRODUCTION

You learned in Chapter 1 that a paragraph is a group of sentences about one topic. A paragraph should have three main parts: a topic sentence, supporting sentences (the body), and a concluding sentence.

In this chapter, you will study each of these parts in more detail. You will also work with and then write paragraphs that use an organization pattern known as listing order. Then you will learn about compound sentences to help you combine your ideas more effectively.

To help you get ideas for your paragraphs, you will first do some prewriting.

## PREWRITING

There are many different prewriting techniques that you can use to get ideas to write about. In this chapter you will use clustering.

### CLUSTERING

**Clustering** is a prewriting technique that allows you to brainstorm and develop your ideas with the help of a diagram called a **cluster**. Here is how to do it.

Begin by writing your topic in the middle of your paper. Draw a circle around it. Then think of ideas related to the topic. Write words or short phrases in circles around the topic and connect them with lines to the main circle. Write down every idea that comes into your mind. Don't stop to worry if an idea is a good one or not.

**Cluster 1**

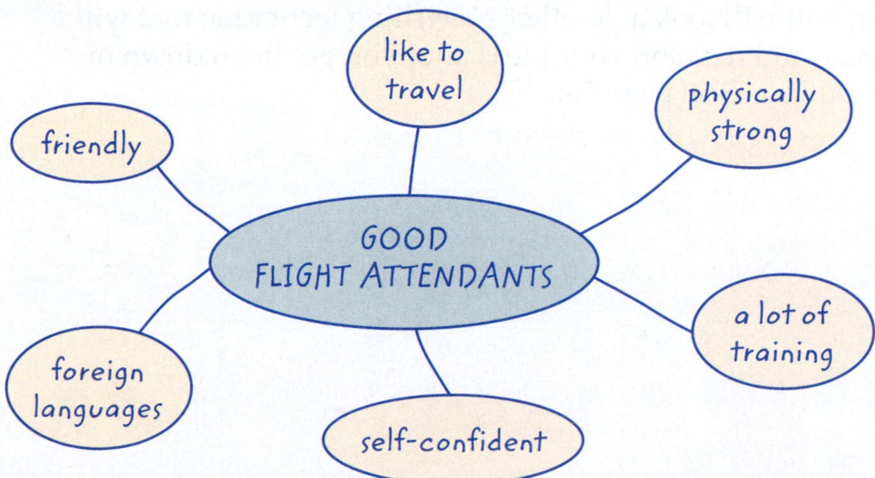

Next, think about the word or phrase in each circle, and add ideas that are related to it. As before, draw circles around each idea and draw lines to connect the ideas. From these clusters, or groups of circles, you can begin to see which ideas to use and which to delete. Keep the clusters that have the most circles, and cross out the ones that didn't produce related ideas.

**Cluster 2**

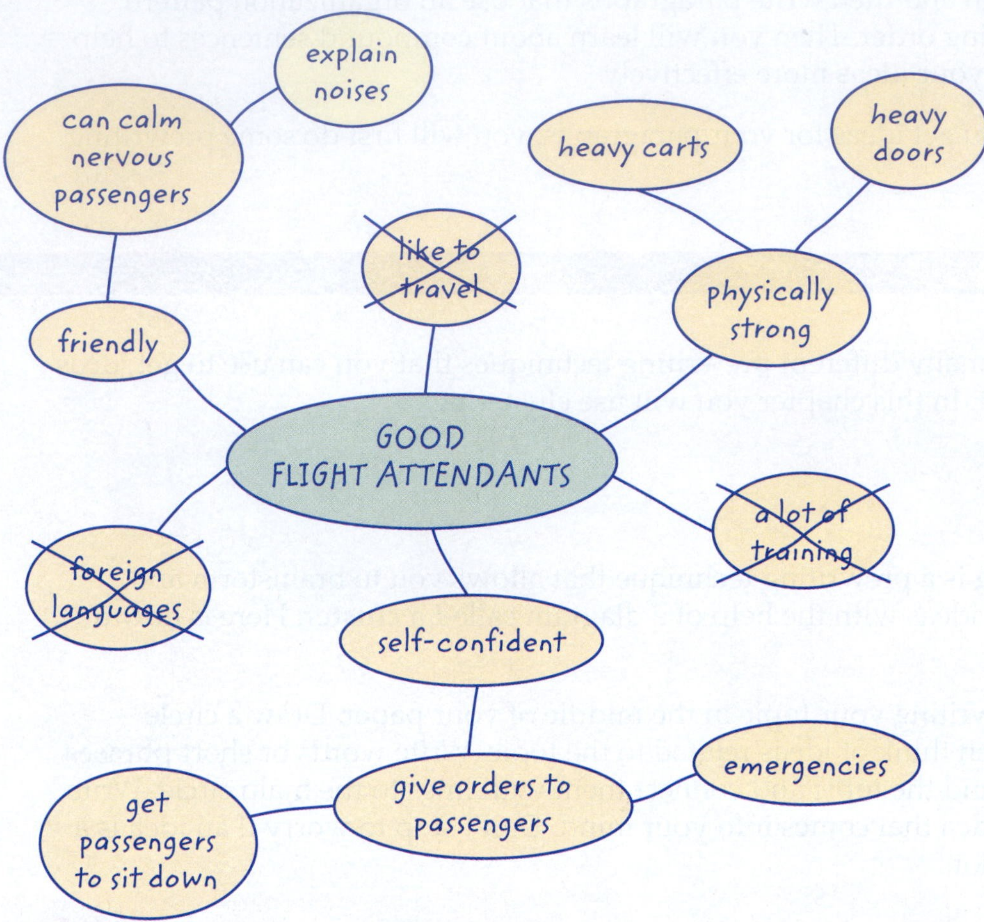


Later in the chapter, you will look at another prewriting technique that will help you further organize and develop your ideas after you get them down on paper in a cluster (see Outlining on page 56).

**PRACTICE 1** **Using Clustering to Get Ideas**

**A** Create a cluster for a job you have or would like to have. Use the chart to give you ideas about the characteristics and abilities that the job requires.

| Characteristics and Abilities | | |
|---|---|---|
| **Adjectives** | **Nouns** | **Phrases** |
| creative | creativity | can give clear instructions |
| dedicated | dedication | can manage people well |
| dependable | dependability | has good communication skills |
| enthusiastic | enthusiasm | is a good public speaker |
| friendly | friendliness | is good at math |
| intelligent | intelligence | is willing to work hard |
| knowledgeable | knowledge | likes traveling |
| organized | organization | works well with children |
| patient | patience | works well with coworkers |
| self-confident | self-confidence | writes well |

**B** Share your cluster with a partner. Discuss ways to expand it. Then talk about which ideas you might want to cut out. You will use this cluster in the Try It Out! activity on page 57.

## LISTING-ORDER PARAGRAPHS

Organization is one of the most important writing skills. A well-organized paragraph is easy to read and understand because the ideas are in a recognizable pattern. Listing order is one of the patterns that writers often use in English. In a listing-order paragraph, you divide the topic into separate points. In the paragraph, you discuss one point, then another point, then a third point, and so on.

There are three keys to writing a listing-order paragraph:

- Begin with a topic sentence that names the topic and says it has several points.
- Write about (or list) each point separately.
- End with a concluding sentence that reminds the reader about the points just discussed.

## LOOKING AT THE MODEL

The writing model is about qualities that good flight attendants have.

**Work with a partner or in a small group. Read the model. Then answer the questions.**

### Writing Model

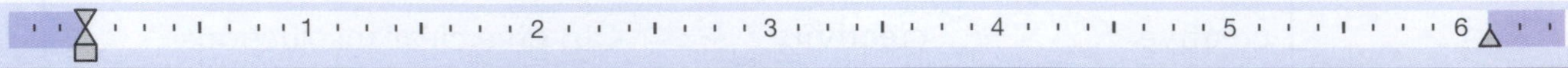

### Good Flight Attendants

Good flight attendants have three important characteristics. First of all, they are very friendly. They enjoy greeting passengers and making them feel comfortable. Sometimes passengers are quite afraid of flying. Friendly flight attendants are good at talking to them and helping them feel calm. For example, they can explain strange noises made by the aircraft. Second, good flight attendants are self-confident. They can give clear instructions to passengers, and they must be rather firm so that passengers obey them. This characteristic is especially important in emergencies. Third, good flight attendants are fairly strong. They have to push heavy carts of food and drinks up and down the aisles. They also have to open and close the airplane's extremely heavy doors. In short, good flight attendants are friendly, self-confident, and strong.

#### Questions about the Model

1. Look at the title. What is the topic of the paragraph?
2. Look at the first sentence. What does it say about the topic?
3. How many characteristics should the reader look for in this paragraph? What are they?
4. What information does the last sentence repeat?

### Looking at Vocabulary: Intensifiers

We can describe how strong a characteristic is by using words like *very* and *extremely*.

He is a **very** hard worker.

She is **fairly** good at the job.

They are **exceptionally** skilled.

We are **quite** sure about it.

These words are known as **intensifiers** because they intensify (or strengthen) the meaning of the words they describe. The diagram shows the relative weakness and strength of these intensifiers:

**INTENSIFIERS**

| *Weaker* | → | → | → | → | *Stronger* |
|---|---|---|---|---|---|
| fairly | rather | quite | very | especially | extremely |

**PRACTICE 2** **Looking at Intensifiers**

**A** **Look at the intensifiers in the diagram above. Find and underline them in the writing model. Then circle the word that each one intensifies.**

First of all, they are very friendly.

**B** **Use a variety of intensifiers from the diagram above to complete these sentences about yourself.**

1. I am ___very___ creative.
2. I am __________ talkative.
3. I am __________ organized.
4. I am __________ funny.
5. I am __________ strong.
6. I am __________ patient.
7. I am __________ good at cooking.
8. I am __________ good at math.

**C** **Discuss your sentences from Part B with a partner. Give examples of each characteristic you describe.**

1. I am very creative. I want to be a graphic designer someday. I love to paint and draw in my spare time.

## ORGANIZATION

In Chapter 1, you learned that a paragraph has three parts: a topic sentence, supporting sentences, and a concluding sentence. Now you will study each part of a paragraph in more detail.

### THE TOPIC SENTENCE

The most important sentence in a paragraph is the **topic sentence**. It is called the topic sentence because it tells readers what the main idea of the paragraph is. In other words, it tells readers what they are going to read about. The topic sentence is usually the first sentence in a paragraph. It is the top piece of bread in our paragraph "sandwich."

A topic sentence has two parts: 1) a **topic**, which tells what the paragraph will be about, and 2) a **controlling idea**, which tells what the paragraph will say about the topic. It tells the reader: This paragraph will discuss these things—and only these things—about this topic.

For example, the topic of the writing model on page 38 is *good flight attendants*. What will the paragraph say about good flight attendants? The controlling idea tells us: *They have three important characteristics*. The paragraph will not talk about their uniforms, their training, or their duties. It will only discuss three important characteristics that good flight attendants have.

Here are examples of topic sentences about English:

English is constantly adding new words.

English borrows words from other languages.

English is necessary for many different jobs.

Note that the topic in each of these examples is the same (*English*), but the controlling ideas are different. That means that each paragraph will discuss something very different about English.

In the topic sentence, the topic can come before or after the controlling idea:

BEFORE: English (TOPIC) borrows words from other languages. (CONTROLLING IDEA)

AFTER: Other languages give words to (CONTROLLING IDEA) English. (TOPIC)

BEFORE: English (TOPIC) is necessary for many different jobs. (CONTROLLING IDEA)

AFTER: Many different jobs require (CONTROLLING IDEA) English. (TOPIC)

## PRACTICE 3 Analyzing Topic Sentences

**Look at each group of topic sentences. Circle the topic and underline the controlling idea of each sentence. (You will use these groups of sentences again later.)**

### Group 1

1. Good roommates have four characteristics.
2. College students face many challenges.
3. Living with your parents has certain advantages.
4. Successful student athletes have several characteristics.
5. Small colleges are better than big universities for several reasons.

### Group 2

1. Successful managers share several characteristics.
2. New teachers must master several skills.
3. Living with your parents has certain disadvantages.
4. Good test-takers share several characteristics.
5. Big universities are better than small ones for three reasons.

## PRACTICE 4 Recognizing Topic Sentences

Find the topic sentence in each paragraph. Circle the topic and underline the controlling idea.

**PARAGRAPH 1**

### Libraries

Libraries offer people a wide variety of activities. Reading, of course, is one of the main activities. People browse the shelves to find interesting books to borrow, and they also come to read newspapers and magazines. Using computers is another popular activity. People can read articles online or do research. They can also check their email, shop, or contact their friends on social networking sites. Studying is also a popular activity. Many students come to the library after school to do their homework or study for tests. Some libraries even have areas where students can study together and talk quietly. Indeed, libraries are for much more than simply reading books.

**PARAGRAPH 2**

### Libraries

Libraries are busy from morning until night in my city. In the morning, you can find retired people and others who aren't working. Some come to borrow books, read newspapers and magazines, and use the computers. Others bring their preschool children in order to read to them or to take part in story hours. In the afternoon, students come to the library. They use the computers, do their homework, or work together on assignments. In the evening, the library is also quite busy. People come to relax after work, and families often visit after dinner. In short, people use libraries all day long for a variety of reasons.

**Paragraph 3**

### Libraries

A good place to volunteer in your community is a library. First, libraries use volunteers to sort and put books back on the shelves. You can learn how to do this with only a few hours of training. Second, some libraries use volunteers to help people use the computers. You can help people learn how to find information and send emails. In addition, libraries often use volunteers to help out in the children's area. You can lead story hours or help children with special art and reading projects. Finally, libraries use volunteers as tutors. For example, you can volunteer to help students with their homework or become a conversation partner for someone learning English. To sum up, libraries welcome many different kinds of volunteers.

**Paragraph 4**

### Libraries

Over the past 20 years, many changes have taken place in libraries. First of all, libraries now have computers for people to use. Usually, there is no charge to use the computer for research or for surfing online. Second, there are fewer records, cassette tapes, and video tapes. These have been replaced by CDs and DVDs. In addition, many libraries now have a kiosk where you can check out your books using a computer. Finally, libraries have become more social and community-oriented than they were in the past. They are now places where people come to discuss ideas, learn a craft, study with friends, or join a community group. As our world changes and technology improves, libraries continue to change to meet the needs of the people who use them.

## PRACTICE 5 Choosing Topic Sentences

**A** Read the paragraphs. Circle the letter of the best topic sentence for each one and write it on the line.

**PARAGRAPH 1**

Living in a foreign country has a number of benefits.

______________ First, living in a foreign country helps you learn another language faster than studying it at school. Second, you can learn directly about the history, geography, and culture of a country. Third, you become especially knowledgeable about different cultures and different ways of living. Fourth, living in a foreign country makes you appreciate your own country more.

**a.** Living in a foreign country helps you learn.
**b.** Everyone should live in a foreign country for a while.
**c.** Living in a foreign country has a number of benefits.

**PARAGRAPH 2**

______________________________

______________ Some colleges and universities in the United States are private. Private colleges and universities do not get money from taxes, so they are usually more expensive. Other colleges and universities are public; that is, the citizens of each state pay some of the costs through their taxes. As a result, public colleges are cheaper for students to attend. No matter which type of college you attend—public or private—you can get a good education.

**a.** There are two main types of colleges and universities in the United States.
**b.** Public colleges and universities get money from taxes.
**c.** There are many colleges and universities in the United States.

**Paragraph 3**

______________________________________________

______________________ One reason for choosing a small college is that classes are small. The average class in a small college is 20 students. Another reason is that it is fairly easy to meet with professors. Professors in small colleges have time to help students and are usually happy to do so. In addition, small colleges are friendly, so new students make friends quickly. For these three reasons, small colleges are better than large universities for many students.

**a.** Small colleges are friendlier than large universities.
**b.** There are several reasons for attending a small college instead of a large university.
**c.** You can get an excellent education at a small college.

**Paragraph 4**

______________________________________________

______________________ First of all, employers want workers to be dependable. That is, they want workers who come to work every day. Second, employers want workers who are quite responsible. Can the boss give the worker a project to do and know that it will be done well? Third, employers look for workers who can work well with others. The ability to get along with coworkers is extremely important to the success of a business. To summarize, employers look for dependable, responsible team players.

**a.** It is difficult to find good employees these days.
**b.** Employers read job applications very carefully.
**c.** Employers look for three main qualities in their employees.

**B** Read the paragraphs. Then write a topic sentence for each one.

**Paragraph 1**

Colleges and universities in the United States offer several different types of degrees. An associate's degree is given for a two-year program of study. Most students at a community college earn an associate's degree. Students at a four-year college or university earn an undergraduate degree, also called a bachelor of arts (BA) or bachelor of science (BS). Some students continue their studies by doing postgraduate work at a university. After several years, they can receive a graduate degree, such as a master's degree (MA) or a doctorate (Ph.D., doctor in philosophy). In short, there are several types of college degrees in the United States.

**Paragraph 2**

______________________________________________

______________________ First, good teachers know their subject extremely well. That is, a math teacher has advanced education in mathematics, and an English teacher knows a lot about English grammar. Second, good teachers are especially good communicators. This means they know how to present information in ways that students can understand. Third, good teachers are enthusiastic. That is, they can show students that they are interested in their subject and that the subject is quite fun to learn about. To summarize, good teachers have expert knowledge, good communication skills, and enthusiasm for their subject.

**Paragraph 3**

______________________________________________

______________________ The first type of shopper doesn't like to waste time. She knows what she wants to buy and how much she wants to pay. If the store has what she wants, she buys it and leaves. She is a good kind of customer because she doesn't take too much of a salesperson's time. A second type of shopper comes into a store with a general idea of what she wants, listens to the salesperson's suggestions, looks at a few items, and makes a decision. She is also a good kind of customer. A third kind of shopper has no idea what she wants. She spends two hours trying to decide which item to buy. She takes up a lot of a salesperson's time and sometimes doesn't buy anything. In conclusion, the first two types of shoppers are a salesperson's dream, but the third type is a salesperson's nightmare.

## SUPPORTING SENTENCES

**Supporting sentences** follow the topic sentence in a paragraph. Supporting sentences explain or prove the ideas in the topic sentence. They are the "filling" in a paragraph "sandwich." The supporting sentences are the biggest part of a paragraph, just as the filling is the biggest part of a sandwich.

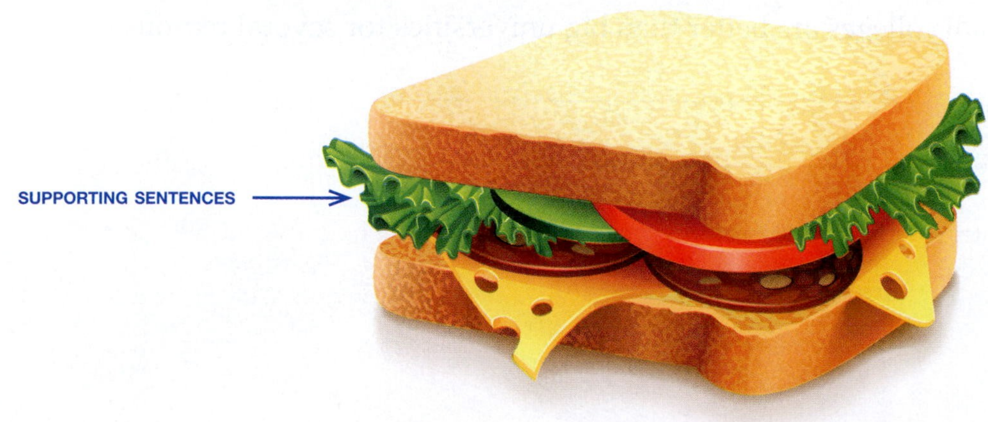

**PRACTICE 6** **Supporting Sentences**

Work alone or with a partner. Add supporting points for the topic sentences in Group 1 from Practice 3 on page 41. Write your points in the spaces provided. You may write phrases or sentences.

1. Good roommates have four characteristics.

   a. are neat, tidy

   b. are cheerful

   c. share housework

   d. pay their share of the rent on time

2. College students face many challenges.

   a. ______________________

   b. ______________________

   c. ______________________

3. Living with your parents has certain advantages.

   a. ______________________

   b. ______________________

   c. ______________________

4. Successful student athletes have several characteristics.

   a. ______________________

   b. ______________________

   c. ______________________

5. Small colleges are better than big universities for several reasons.

   a. ______________________

   b. ______________________

   c. ______________________

## LISTING-ORDER TRANSITION SIGNALS

To show readers that they are moving from one supporting idea to another, good writers use words or phrases known as **transition signals**. A transition signal alerts the reader that the writer is moving on to the next supporting idea. It also shows how the new supporting idea is related to the previous idea.

In a listing-order paragraph, you can use transition signals such as *First*, *Second*, and *Third* to show the reader the order of the main points.

Here are some transition signals that show listing order:

| Listing-Order Transition Signals | |
|---|---|
| First, | . . . also . . . |
| First of all, | . . . , also. |
| Second, | |
| Third, | |
| In addition, | |
| Also, | |
| Finally, | |

Most listing-order transition signals come at the beginning of the sentence, followed by a comma.

> **First,** living in a foreign country helps you learn another language faster than studying it at school.
>
> **In addition,** small colleges are friendlier, so new students make friends more quickly.
>
> **Also,** studying is a popular library activity.

The transition signal *also* is an exception. You can use it at the beginning of a sentence with a comma (as in the example above), but you can also use it with a verb (without a comma) or at the end of a sentence (preceded by a comma).

> Studying is **also** a popular library activity.
>
> Students **also** like to study in the library.
>
> Studying is a popular library activity**, also**.

**PRACTICE 7** **Listing-Order Transition Signals**

**A** **Find the listing-order transition signals in the writing model on page 38. Then fill in the blanks.**

1. Transition signal for the first main point: ____________________
2. Transition signal for the second main point: ____________________
3. Transition signal for the third main point: ____________________
4. What other listing-order transition signal appears in the model?

____________________

**B** **Complete the paragraph with listing-order transition signals. Add commas where needed. For some, there may be more than one answer.**

### Kinds of Intelligence[1]

There are many kinds of intelligence. ____________ (1.) there is mathematical-logical intelligence. People with this kind of intelligence become mathematicians, scientists, and engineers. ____________ (2.) there is linguistic[2] intelligence. People with linguistic intelligence are good at language, so many become musicians and writers. We are familiar with these first two kinds of intelligence, but other kinds are not so familiar. There are ____________ (3.) spatial intelligence and musical intelligence. Spatial intelligence is necessary for architects and artists, and musical intelligence is necessary for musicians. ____________ (4.) there is kinesthetic[3] intelligence. Athletes and dancers have kinesthetic intelligence. Personal intelligence is a kind of intelligence ____________ (5.). People with personal intelligence manage people well, so they become leaders of society. In short, there is more than one way to be smart.

[1] This paragraph is based on the work of Howard Gardner, a professor at the Harvard Graduate School of Education.

[2] **linguistic:** related to language

[3] **kinesthetic:** related to movement of the human body

## Unity

Unity is an important characteristic of a well-written paragraph. When a paragraph has unity, all the sentences in it are about one main idea. Another way of saying this is that all the supporting sentences must be **relevant**, which means "directly related to the main idea." For example, if your paragraph is about your mother's good cooking, a sentence such as *My sister is also a good cook* is **irrelevant** (that is, not relevant) because the paragraph is about your mother, not your sister. When you write a paragraph, make sure that all of your supporting sentences are relevant.

### PRACTICE 8 Editing for Unity

**Work alone or with a partner. Each paragraph contains two irrelevant sentences. Circle the topic and underline the controlling idea in each topic sentence. Then draw a line through each irrelevant sentence.**

**PARAGRAPH 1**

**Boston**

Boston is one of the most popular U.S. cities with college students. There are two main reasons for this. First, students enjoy being in a city that is full of other college students. The Boston area has over 50 colleges and universities, including Boston University, Massachusetts Institute of Technology, and Harvard University. The Charles River, between Boston and Cambridge, is famous for boating and races. Because of the large number of college students, there are many events and activities in the city every day. Second, Boston has the feel of a big city, but it's really rather small. It is quite convenient for students to get around using public transportation. It is very easy for students to become familiar with the city and feel comfortable. There are many friendly neighborhoods near the colleges, and students usually feel welcomed. However, some Boston residents complain about noisy or irresponsible college students. It's no surprise that people regard Boston as one of the top U.S. college towns.

*(continued on next page)*

**Paragraph 2**

### Nurses

Good nurses should have at least five characteristics. First, they must be caring. They must show genuine concern for sick, injured, or frightened people. Second, nurses must be extremely organized. If a nurse forgets to give a patient his or her medicine on time, the consequences could be serious. Third, nurses must be quite calm. They may have to make a life-and-death decision in an emergency, and it's clear that calm people make better decisions than anxious people. Doctors also need to stay calm in emergencies. In addition, nurses should be physically strong because nursing requires a lot of hard physical work. Finally, they must be intelligent enough to learn difficult subjects such as chemistry and psychology and to operate the complex equipment used in hospitals today. There is a shortage of nurses today, so they earn good salaries. In brief, nursing is a profession for people who are caring, organized, calm, strong, and intelligent.

## THE CONCLUDING SENTENCE

Paragraphs that stand alone (that is, paragraphs that are not part of a longer composition) often end with a **concluding sentence**. A concluding sentence signals the close of the paragraph to the reader.

Here are several points to keep in mind about concluding sentences:

- Sometimes a concluding sentence reminds the reader of the main point by restating the topic sentence in different words.

  In short, there are several types of college degrees in the United States.

  It's no surprise that people regard Boston as one of the top U.S. college towns.

- Sometimes a concluding sentence summarizes the main points.

  To summarize, employers look for dependable, responsible team players.

  In brief, nursing is a profession for people who are caring, organized, calm, strong, and intelligent.

- Writers often use a **conclusion signal** to show their readers that this is the end of the paragraph. The chart lists several conclusion signals. Notice that there is always a comma after a conclusion signal.

| Conclusion Signals | | |
|---|---|---|
| To conclude,<br>In conclusion, | To sum up,<br>To summarize,<br>In summary, | In brief,<br>In short,<br>Indeed, |

**Writing Tip**

Never introduce a new idea in your concluding sentence. Instead, review or repeat the ideas you have already discussed.

**DO THIS:** In short, good flight attendants are friendly, self-confident, and strong.

**DO NOT DO THIS:** Also, good flight attendants love to travel.

**OR**

In conclusion, I hope to become a good flight attendant some day.

**PRACTICE 9** **Choosing Concluding Sentences**

**Read the paragraphs. Circle the letter of the best concluding sentence for each one, and write it on the line.**

**PARAGRAPH 1**

There are two reasons I love big cities. First of all, big cities are alive 24 hours a day. You can go shopping, see a movie, exercise at a gym, get something to eat, or go roller skating at any time of the day or night. Second, in big cities you are free to do whatever you like. No one watches your daily comings and goings. You can stay out all night or stay home all day, and no one will judge you. ______________________________

______________________________

**a.** To sum up, I love big cities because you can be independent.

**b.** In short, big cities attract me because there are so many things to do.

**c.** In brief, I like big cities because of their energy and freedom.

**PARAGRAPH 2**

There are two reasons I hate big cities. First of all, big cities are noisy 24 hours a day. You can hear horns honking, traffic roaring, music blaring, and people talking at all hours. It is never quiet in a big city. Second, there is no feeling of community in big cities. No one knows or cares about you. Neighbors who have lived next door to each other for many years don't even know each others' names. That can make life extremely lonely. ______________________________

______________________________

**a.** In brief, big cities are noisy, lonely places to live.

**b.** In conclusion, I prefer to live in a small town, where it is quieter and people are friendlier.

**c.** Also, big cities have a lot of crime.

## PRACTICE 10 Writing Concluding Sentences

**A** Read the paragraphs. Write a concluding sentence for each one.

### Paragraph 1

Successful young fashion designers usually have three characteristics. First of all, they must be very creative. They must use their artistic abilities and their knowledge of textiles and colors. Second, they must be willing to work hard over a long period of time. Usually, young fashion designers start out as poorly paid assistants or as unpaid interns. They must work many long hours for little or no pay to learn the needed skills. Finally, successful young fashion designers must be well-organized and understand the importance of building an outstanding portfolio. A portfolio is a large folder with sketches, photos, and samples of a designer's work. It is visual proof of a designer's talent, vision, and accomplishments. ______________________________

______________________________

### Paragraph 2

I find that being a computer salesperson is a very rewarding job. First, my job allows me to meet many different types of people. I like this because I'm an outgoing person, and I enjoy talking with people and finding out about them. Second, my job requires me to problem-solve and find creative ways to meet my customers' needs. I find it satisfying to figure out which of my company's products are best for my clients. Third, the job requires me to learn about new developments in my field. I find this part of the job satisfying because I like staying informed, and I love the challenge of learning new things. ______________________________

______________________________

**B** In Practice 6 on page 48, you wrote supporting ideas for five topic sentences. Now, write a concluding sentence for each topic. Use a different conclusion signal for each.

1. *To sum up, neatness, cheerfulness, helpfulness, and financial responsibility are qualities of good roommates.*

2. ______________________________

3. ______________________________

4. ______________________________

5. ______________________________

## OUTLINING

In the Prewriting section of this chapter (pages 35–36), you saw how clustering helps you get ideas about a topic. Once you have your ideas, you can use another prewriting technique known as **outlining** to help you organize them.

Here is the outline created from the edited cluster about good flight attendants on page 36:

| | |
|---|---|
| TITLE | *Good Flight Attendants* |
| TOPIC SENTENCE | *Good flight attendants have three important characteristics.* |
| 1ST MAIN POINT | *A. Friendly* |
| 2ND MAIN POINT | *B. Self-confident* |
| 3RD MAIN POINT | *C. Physically strong* |
| CONCLUDING SENTENCE | *In short, good flight attendants are friendly, self-confident, and strong.* |

To create the outline, the writer took the three main characteristics that he identified in his cluster and wrote them down in the order that he wanted to write about them. He labeled these A, B, and C. To complete the outline, he added a topic sentence and a concluding sentence.

**Writing Tip**

When you make an outline, try to make the main points (A, B, C, and so on) grammatically the same—all adjectives, all nouns, all verb phrases, or all sentences.

## PRACTICE 11 Outlining

**Use your cluster in Practice 1 on page 37 to complete the outline. Find three main points and fill in the A, B, and C blanks. Then add a title, a topic sentence, and the concluding sentence.**

| | |
|---|---|
| TITLE | |
| TOPIC SENTENCE | |
| 1ST MAIN POINT | A. |
| 2ND MAIN POINT | B. |
| 3RD MAIN POINT | C. |
| CONCLUDING SENTENCE | |

**TRY IT OUT!** **On a separate sheet of paper, write a paragraph using the outline you created in Practice 11. Use the writing model on page 38 as a guide. Follow these directions:**

1. Follow your outline as you write your draft.
2. Add details to support each characteristic or ability. Write two or three sentences for each main point.
3. Use a variety of intensifiers.
4. Introduce each main point with a listing-order transition signal.
5. Proofread your paragraph and correct any mistakes.

## SENTENCE STRUCTURE

In Chapter 1, you learned about simple sentences. In this chapter, you will look at **compound sentences**.

## COMPOUND SENTENCES

A **compound sentence** is two simple sentences connected by a comma and a coordinating conjunction. Here are some examples:

| SIMPLE SENTENCE | COORDINATING CONJUNCTION | SIMPLE SENTENCE |
|---|---|---|
| My sister is good at math, | **and** | she always gets good grades. |
| I'm also good at math, | **but** | my sister is better than I am. |
| I will ask my teacher for help, | **or** | I will talk to my advisor. |
| My sister is older than I am, | **so** | maybe she can help me. |

Command sentences can also be compound. Remember that the subject *you* is not expressed in commands.

| COMMAND | COORDINATING CONJUNCTION | COMMAND |
|---|---|---|
| (You) Pay attention in class, | **and** | (you) do all of the homework. |
| (You) Listen carefully in class, | **but** | (you) don't be afraid to ask questions. |

Here are three important points to know about compound sentences:

- A comma and a coordinating conjunction connect the two halves of a compound sentence.
- There are seven coordinating conjunctions in English: *for*, *and*, *nor*, *but*, *or*, *yet*, and *so*. Remember them by the phrase "fan boys." In this book, you will practice using the four most common of them: *and*, *but*, *or*, and *so*.
- Don't confuse a compound sentence with a simple sentence that has a compound verb. In the chart, the first sentence in each pair of sentences is simple and doesn't need a comma. The second one is compound and requires a comma.

| SENTENCE TYPE | EXAMPLE | PATTERN |
|---|---|---|
| Simple sentence with compound verb | Tom is good at languages and learns new words easily. | S V V |
| Compound sentence | Tom is good at languages, so I sometimes ask him about words. | S V, *so* S V |

| Sentence type | Example | Pattern |
|---|---|---|
| Simple sentence with compound verb | Last year I tried to learn Arabic but decided it was too difficult for me. | S V V |
| Compound sentence | Last year Tom and I were in the same Arabic class, but I decided to drop the class. | S S V, *but* S V |
| Simple sentence with compound verb | Next year I will find an online Arabic course or perhaps hire a tutor. | S V V |
| Compound sentence | Next year Tom will take another Arabic class, or perhaps he will join a conversation group. | S V, *or* S V |

**PRACTICE 12** **Identifying Simple and Compound Sentences**

**A** Look at the sentences. In each sentence, underline the subjects once and the verbs twice. Then, write the sentence type (*simple* or *compound*) and the pattern.

| | Sentence Type | Pattern |
|---|---|---|
| 1. The summers were hot and humid in my childhood hometown. | simple | S V |
| 2. Every evening it was too hot to sleep, so my sisters and I played outside until dark. | compound | S V, so S S V |
| 3. Our parents sat on the grass and watched. | simple | S V V |
| 4. We played games such as hide-and-seek and tag, or we just sat on the grass and told stories. | compound | S V, or S V V |
| 5. We also caught fireflies. | simple | S V |
| 6. We put the fireflies into a glass jar, and our father punched air holes in the metal lid. | compound | S V, and S V |
| 7. My sisters were afraid of most bugs, but they loved fireflies. | compound | S V, but S V |
| 8. We usually went to bed at nine o'clock, but sometimes we stayed up later. | compound | S V, but S V |
| 9. Around ten o'clock, our mother and father told us to come inside. | simple | S S V |
| 10. We always left the fireflies outside, and we brought our jars into the house. | compound | S V, and S V |

**B** Read the paragraph. In each sentence, underline the subject(s) once and the verb(s) twice. Then add commas where needed. (HINT: Seven commas are missing.)

### Crime Scene Investigators

1 Crime scene investigators must have several characteristics. 2 First, they can't afford to miss any evidence at a crime scene, so they must be extremely careful. 3 They must try hard to follow the correct methods and they must accurately measure and record their findings. 4 Second, crime scene investigations are complicated so investigators must be quite patient. 5 They must work slowly and correctly and they can't rush to complete a job. 6 Finally, they must be able to communicate well. 7 They need to take detailed notes and turn them into well-written reports so they must have excellent writing skills. 8 They also need to deal with police officers, judges, and lawyers so they must be able to explain things clearly and effectively. 9 Crime scene investigators have very interesting jobs but they must be extremely careful, patient, and skilled at communicating their ideas.

**C** For each sentence from the paragraph in Part B, write *simple* or *compound*. Then write the pattern for each sentence.

| | Sentence type | Pattern |
|---|---|---|
| 1. | simple | S V |
| 2. | compound | S V, so S V |
| 3. | compound | S V, and S V |
| 4. | compound | S V, so S V |
| 5. | compound | S V, and S V |
| 6. | simple | S V |
| 7. | compound | S V, so S V |
| 8. | compound | S V, so S V |
| 9. | compound | S V, but S V |

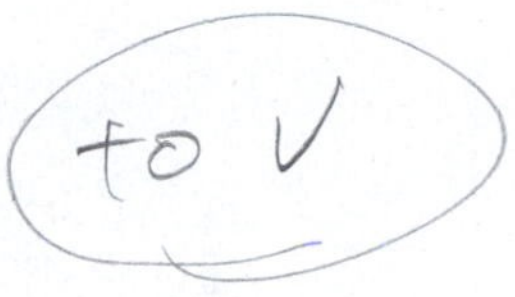

## COORDINATING CONJUNCTIONS: *AND, BUT, OR,* AND *SO*

As mentioned earlier, *and, but, or,* and *so* are the most common coordinating conjunctions. In compound sentences, they have these uses:

| Rules | Examples |
|---|---|
| 1. *And* connects two sentences with similar ideas. The sentences can be positive or negative. | My roommate is an art student, and her brother plays the guitar.<br>She doesn't like rock music, and he doesn't like looking at art. |
| 2. *But* connects two sentences with contrasting or opposite ideas. | She likes classical music, but she doesn't like rock.<br>She likes country music, but he hates it. |
| 3. *Or* connects two sentences that express alternatives or choices. | Every Friday night, she goes to a classical concert, or she visits an art gallery.<br>Every Saturday night, he practices with his band, or he goes to hear a rock concert. |
| 4. *So* connects a reason and a result. | (REASON / RESULT) They both like jazz, so they go to jazz concerts together.<br>(REASON / RESULT) He works a lot, so they don't go out much. |

**PRACTICE 13** Using *And, But, Or,* and *So*

Complete the paragraphs with *and, but, or,* and *so*. For some, there may be more than one answer.

**Paragraph 1**

The waitress said, "Today we have two specials: fried chicken ________ (1.) baked fish." I ordered baked fish, ________ (2.) my friend ordered fried chicken. After 15 minutes, the waitress came back to our table and said, "I made a mistake. We don't have fried chicken ________ (3.) baked fish." I wanted to leave the restaurant immediately, ________ (4.) my friend wanted to stay. He ordered a hamburger ________ (5.) french fries, ________ (6.) I didn't order anything.

**Paragraph 2**

My new neighbors are vegetarians, ________ (1.) they don't eat meat. To be more precise, they don't eat beef, pork, ________ (2.) chicken, ________ (3.) sometimes they eat a little fish. I wanted to be friendly, ________ (4.) I invited them to my house for dinner. They came ________ (5.) brought their young son. He is just a baby, ________ (6.) he can't talk yet. I served fish, rice, ________ (7.) a nice green salad. My neighbors don't drink coffee ________ (8.) tea, ________ (9.) I served lemonade with our meal. For dessert, I offered them a choice of chocolate cake ________ (10.) apple pie. The husband wanted both cake and pie, ________ (11.) the wife didn't want either. They have invited me to come over to their apartment for dinner next month, ________ (12.) they will serve a special vegetarian meal.

**PRACTICE 14** **Writing Compound Sentences**

**A** **Connect each pair of sentences with *and*, *but*, *or*, or *so*. Add a comma as needed. For some, there may be more than one answer.**

1. Canada has two official languages. Everything is printed in both English and French.

   Canada has two official languages, so everything is printed in both English and French.

2. There are several hundred languages in the world. Not all of them have a written form.

3. Chinese is spoken by more people. English is spoken in more countries.

4. There are about one million words in English. Most people use only about ten thousand of them.

5. French used to be the language of international diplomacy. Now it is English.

6. International companies are growing. Bilingual workers are always needed.

7. Young people should know a second language. They will be at a disadvantage in the international job market.

**B** Complete each compound sentence with your own idea.

1. My brother and I are identical twins, but our personalities are very different.
2. We are both tall, and we are both weight ________.
3. He is very creative, but I did not creative ________.
4. I was born a few minutes before my brother, so I am older than my brother.
5. Our mother used to tell us, "Stop fighting, or Not fighting ________."
6. We fought a lot as children, but now we don't fight anyone. ________.

## COMMON SENTENCE ERRORS: RUN-ONS AND COMMA SPLICES

**Run-ons** and **comma splices** are common sentence errors. These errors often occur when there is a close relationship between two sentences.

A run-on is two simple sentences incorrectly joined with no coordinating conjunction and no comma.

RUN-ON: My roommate wants to win the Tour de France someday he spends hours riding his bicycle.

A comma splice is two simple sentences incorrectly joined with a comma but no coordinating conjunction.

INCORRECT: My roommate wants to win the Tour de France someday, he spends hours riding his bicycle.

There are two ways to fix these errors:

- Separate the sentences with a period.

CORRECT: My roommate wants to win the Tour de France someday. He spends hours riding his bicycle.

- Add (or keep) the comma and add a coordinating conjunction.

CORRECT: My roommate wants to win the Tour de France someday, **so** he spends hours riding his bicycle.

## PRACTICE 15 Correcting Run-ons and Comma Splices

Look at the sentences. Write *C* if the sentence is correct. Write *X* if the sentence is incorrect and make corrections. For some, there may be more than one possible correction.

X 1. Some people prefer to work in an office, others prefer to work outdoors.

Some people prefer to work in an office. Others prefer to work outdoors.

OR

Some people prefer to work in an office, but others prefer to work outdoors.

_____ 2. Salespeople are usually very outgoing, they like to talk with people.

_____ 3. Coaches must be enthusiastic and know how to motivate athletes.

_____ 4. News reporters need to work long hours under difficult conditions, the job can be well paid and full of excitement.

_____ 5. Police officers are very dedicated to their jobs, but their lives are often in danger.

_____ 6. Vets need to love animals, they must have excellent people skills, too.

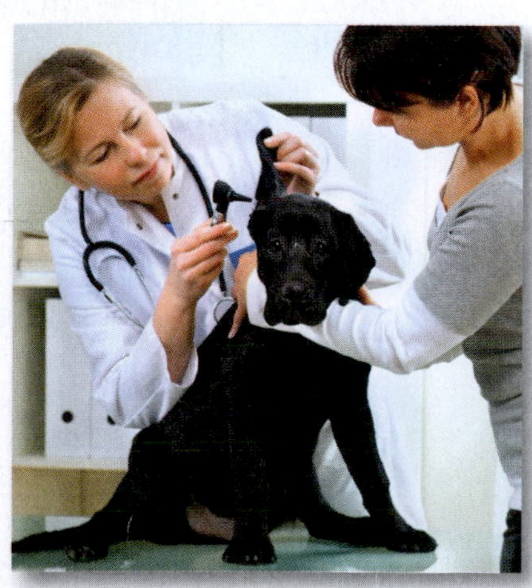

*(continued on next page)*

X 7. Successful politicians are usually very charismatic, voters need to trust them.

Successful politicians are usually very charismatic and voters need to trust them.

X 8. I want to be a psychologist, I have to attend graduate school.

I want to be a psychologist, and I have to attend graduate school.

X 9. Architects can design homes for individuals, they can design buildings for companies.

Architects can design homes for individuals, and they can design buildings for companies.

X 10. Mechanics must work well with their hands, they also need to be good problem solvers.

Mechanics must work well with their hands, and they also need to be good problem solvers.

## Applying Vocabulary: Using Intensifiers

Before you begin your writing assignment, review the words on pages 38–39. Which words do you need more practice with?

## PRACTICE 16 Using Intensifiers

**Think of people you know in different professions. These can be friends, relatives, or famous public figures. Write sentences using the prompts and one of the intensifiers in the diagram.**

| *Weaker* | → | → | → | → | *Stronger* |
|---|---|---|---|---|---|
| fairly | rather | quite | very | especially | extremely |

1. is a good public speaker

   The mayor is an extremely good public speaker.

2. works well with children

3. works well with coworkers

4. is a creative artist

_______________

5. is a talented musician

_______________

6. is organized

_______________

7. is self-confident

_______________

8. is knowledgeable about political events

_______________

## WRITING ASSIGNMENT

Your writing assignment for this chapter will be to write a listing-order paragraph on the topic of a career. Use a topic from Group 2 in Practice 3 on page 41. Use listing order to organize your ideas. Follow the steps in the writing process.

### STEP 1: Prewrite to get ideas.

- Brainstorm ideas by creating a cluster. Follow the procedure on pages 35–36.
- When you are done, study your cluster and choose two to four ideas to write about.
- Make an outline. Use the format on page 56. Your outline should include all three parts of a paragraph: a topic sentence, main points, and a concluding sentence.
- Review the words in Looking at Vocabulary and Applying Vocabulary on pages 38–39 and 66–67. Look at your outline again and, if possible, add in some of these words.

### STEP 2: Write the first draft.

- Write *FIRST DRAFT* at the top of your paper.
- Use a listing-order transition signal to introduce each new main point. Write two or three additional supporting sentences to support each main point. Include at least one compound sentence in your paragraph.
- Use a conclusion signal to introduce the concluding sentence.

### STEP 3: Revise and edit the first draft.

- Exchange papers with a partner and give each other feedback on your paragraphs. Use Chapter 2 Peer Review on page 208.
- Consider your partner's feedback and revise your paragraph. Mark changes on your first draft.
- Check your paragraph carefully against Chapter 2 Writer's Self-Check on page 209, and continue to make changes as necessary.

### STEP 4: Write a new draft.

- Refer to the changes you made on your first draft and do a final draft of your paragraph.
- Proofread it carefully.
- Hand it in to your teacher. Your teacher may also ask you to hand in your prewriting, your outline, and your first draft.

## SELF-ASSESSMENT

**In this chapter, you learned to:**

❍ Use clustering to get ideas for writing

❍ Identify the three parts of a listing-order paragraph

❍ Use listing-order transition signals and conclusion signals

❍ Organize ideas with an outline

❍ Work with compound sentences

❍ Identify and correct run-ons and comma splices

❍ Use listing order to write a paragraph related to a career.

**Which ones can you do well? Mark them ✓**

**Which ones do you need to practice more? Mark them ✗**

# EXPANSION

## TIMED WRITING

To succeed in academic writing you need to be able to write quickly and fluently. For example, you might have to write a paragraph for a test in class, and you only have 30 minutes. In this activity, you will write a paragraph in class. You will have 30 minutes. To complete the activity in time, follow the directions.

1. Read the writing prompt below (or the prompt your teacher assigns) carefully. Make sure you understand the question or task. Then decide on the topic of your paragraph. (3 minutes)
2. Use clustering to get ideas. Decide which ideas you will write about and then make an outline to organize your ideas. (5 minutes)
3. Write your paragraph. Be sure to include a title, a topic sentence, listing-order transition signals, supporting ideas, and a concluding sentence. (15 minutes)
4. Proofread your paragraph. Correct any mistakes. (7 minutes)
5. Give your paper to your teacher.

**Prompt:** Write a listing-order paragraph about a teacher or a boss. What characteristics and abilities made the person memorable? Include examples to support your main ideas.

## YOUR JOURNAL

Continue making entries in your journal. If you cannot think of a topic for a journal entry, try one of these ideas:

- What career or profession are you interested in? Discuss two or three reasons for your interest. Support each reason with examples or explanations.
- Overall, was your high school experience positive or negative? Include three main reasons and support each one with examples or explanations.
- What are the most important characteristics for a friend to have? Write about two or three characteristics and say why they are important.

*For more ideas for journal entries, see Appendix A on page 193.*

CHAPTER 3

# GIVING INSTRUCTIONS

## OBJECTIVES

**Writers need certain skills.**

**In this chapter, you will learn to:**

- Use listing to get ideas for writing
- Organize a "how-to" paragraph using time order or listing order
- Edit a list of ideas to create an outline
- Work with complex sentences with time clauses
- Correct sentence fragments
- Use additional rules for capitalization and commas
- Write, revise, and edit a "how-to" paragraph

*The woman is interviewing the man for a job. What steps do you think each of them took to prepare for the interview?*

## INTRODUCTION

In this chapter, you will learn how to write a clearly organized paragraph that gives instructions. This kind of paragraph is sometimes called a "how-to" paragraph because it explains how to do something or how to make something: for example, how to change a flat tire or how to perform a science experiment.

You will learn how to organize your ideas using time order and time-order transition signals. You will also learn about complex sentences with time clauses so that you can use them to help your reader better understand the process you are writing about.

To help you get ideas for writing, you will first do some prewriting.

## PREWRITING

In Chapters 1 and 2, you practiced several prewriting techniques to help you get ideas for your writing, including asking questions and taking notes, freewriting, clustering, and outlining. In this chapter, you will explore another technique: listing. Later in the chapter you will learn how to create an outline by editing the ideas you get from listing (see pages 83–85).

### LISTING

Just as you might make a shopping list before you go to the supermarket or a "to do" list to help you organize a busy day, you can also make a list of ideas to help you generate ideas for writing. Like freewriting and clustering, **listing** is a brainstorming activity. You simply begin by thinking about your topic. Then you make a list of every word or phrase that comes into your mind. Don't stop to wonder if an idea is good or if your spelling or grammar is correct. Just keep writing down words and phrases in list form until you run out of ideas.

## PRACTICE 1 Using Listing to Get Ideas

Work in a small group. Look at the two photographs (below and on page 73). Choose the one that you think you can write about in more detail. Make a list of everything you should do to wash the car or make a pizza with your favorite topping. Write down every idea. Don't worry about writing complete sentences or putting your ideas in order. You will use this list in Practice 6 on page 85.

**How to Wash a Car**

*Collect sponges, rags, bucket, soap*

**How to Make a Delicious Pizza**

*List of ingredients for dough and toppings*

## "HOW-TO" PARAGRAPHS

A "how-to" paragraph explains how to do something or how to make something. In order to give a clear explanation, a "how-to" paragraph must be carefully organized. There are four keys to writing a clear "how-to" paragraph.

- Begin with a topic sentence that names the topic and says the paragraph will give instructions about it.
- Divide the instructions into a series of steps or tips. For some topics, you will need to use **time order** and **time-order transition signals** to present each step of a process from beginning to end. For example, you would use time order to give step-by-step instructions on how to check the oil in a car.

  **First,** turn off the engine. **Next,** open the hood of the car. **After you've done that,** locate the . . .

  For topics where it is not important to do steps in a certain order, you can use **listing order** and **listing-order transition signals** to present a series of tips. (You studied listing-order paragraphs in Chapter 2.) For instance, you could use listing order to present a series of tips on how to improve your speaking skills.

  **First,** use every opportunity to practice. . . . **Second,** don't worry about making mistakes. . . . **In addition,** . . .

- Explain each step or tip one by one.
- Use transition signals to introduce each important step or tip.

## LOOKING AT THE MODEL

The writing model explains how to have a successful yard sale.

**Work with a partner or in a small group. Read the model. Then answer the questions.**

**Writing Model**

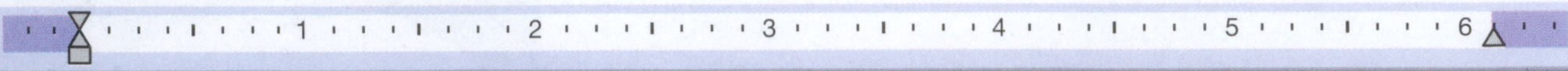

### How to Have a Successful Yard Sale

1 In order to have a successful yard sale, you need to prepare well by following these simple steps. 2 First, decide on a day and time for your sale. 3 Make sure it's several weeks in the future so that you have time to get ready. 4 Next, look through your family's belongings and collect used items in good condition. 5 These can be anything that you no longer want, such as clothing, toys, books, dishes, lamps, furniture, and even TVs. 6 Then clean everything thoroughly, and clearly label each item with a price. 7 If you are not sure how much to charge, check the prices at other yard sales in your community. 8 If you price your items cheaply, people will be more likely to buy them. 9 After that, you should store your items carefully until the day of the sale. 10 About a week before, get some change from the bank. 11 You should get at least $20 in one-dollar bills, $50 in five-dollar bills, $100 in 10-dollar bills, and one or two rolls of quarters. 12 A day or two before the sale, make signs advertising the date, time, and address of your sale. 13 Then put the signs up in places where they will easily attract people's attention. 14 Finally, on the morning of the sale, get up early and arrange the items attractively on tables in front of your home. 15 It's important to be ready on time because smart shoppers often arrive early. 16 If you work hard and organize the details, your yard sale will be a great success.

### Questions about the Model

1. What is the topic?
2. Which sentence tells you the topic? What is this sentence called?
3. Does the writer use time order or listing order?
4. What transition signals and time phrases does the writer use? Put a dotted line under them. (HINT: There are eight in all ranging from one to seven words.)
5. Writers often use commands in "how-to" paragraphs. Sentence 2 is a good example ("First, *decide* . . ."). Can you find eight more?

## Looking at Vocabulary: Descriptive Adverbs

When you write a "how-to" paragraph, you will often want to describe the way or manner in which your readers need to do something. For instance, when you instruct readers to clean something, it helps to add a descriptive word that tells *how* to do this:

You don't want to break the glass, so clean the mirror **gently**.

Clean everything **well** because nobody wants to buy dusty items.

When you clean pots and pans, you may have to rub **hard** to remove all the old, built-up grease.

Words like this are known as **adverbs of manner** because they describe the way or manner that someone performs an action. They are useful because they make it clear how you want your readers to perform the actions you describe.

Like other adverbs, most adverbs of manner are formed by adding *-ly* to an adjective. Notice these examples from the model:

attractive**ly** clear**ly**

careful**ly** easi**ly**

cheap**ly** thorough**ly**

Note that some adjectives are irregular and do not add *-ly* to form the adverb. Here are two examples from the model:

well (adverb form of *good*)

hard (adverb form of *hard*)

**PRACTICE 2** **Looking at Words that Describe How to Do Things**

**A** Look at these sentences from the writing model on page 74. Underline the adverbs of manner. Then circle the actions that they describe. (HINT: One sentence has two adverbs of manner.)

1. In order to have a successful yard sale, you need to prepare well by following these simple steps.
2. Then clean everything thoroughly, and clearly label each item with a price.
3. If you price your items cheaply, people will be more likely to buy them.
4. After that, you should store your items carefully until the day of the sale.
5. Then put the signs up in places where they will easily attract people's attention.

*(continued on next page)*

6. Finally, on the morning of the sale, get up early and arrange the items attractively on tables in front of your home.
7. If you work hard and organize the details, your yard sale will be a great success.

**B** **Use the words in the box to complete the sentences.**

| | | | |
|---|---|---|---|
| attractively | cheaply | easily | thoroughly |
| carefully | clearly | hard | well |

1. If you want to play the piano ______________, you will have to practice several hours a day.
2. Study hard, and you will pass the test ______________.
3. Speak slowly and ______________ so your listeners can understand each word.
4. Make sure the paint dries ______________ before you apply a second coat.
5. Winter driving can be dangerous. The first rule to remember is to drive ______________.
6. It isn't easy to live ______________ in a big city, but here are some ways that you can save money.
7. Press down ______________, and continue to press for at least a minute.
8. Here are some tips on how to decorate your apartment ______________ but inexpensively.

## ORGANIZATION

In this section, you will look at how to organize "how-to" paragraphs. You will learn how to write effective topic and concluding sentences and how to use time order and time-order transition signals.

## TOPIC SENTENCES AND CONCLUDING SENTENCES

The topic sentence for a "how-to" paragraph names the topic. The controlling idea part tells your readers that they will learn how to do or make something related to the topic. For example, the first sentence of the writing model names the topic: *a successful yard sale*. It also explains what the paragraph will say about it: *you need to prepare well by following a number of simple steps.*

Here are other examples of topic sentences for "how-to" paragraphs. Notice that they use expressions such as *by taking these steps*, *if you follow my advice*, and *follow these instructions*. Expressions like this tell your reader that this is a "how-to" paragraph.

> Anyone can change a flat tire by taking these steps.
>
> It's easy to soothe a crying baby if you follow my advice.
>
> Follow these instructions to make delicious pizza.

The concluding sentence of a "how-to" paragraph mentions the topic again to remind the reader what the paragraph was about.

> In no time at all, your flat tire will be repaired, and you will be on your way again.
>
> If you follow these four steps, your baby will fall asleep quickly.
>
> You now have a delicious pizza to enjoy.

**PRACTICE 3** **Writing Topic Sentences for "How-To" Paragraphs**

**Work alone or with a partner. Use a phrase from the box to fill in the first blank in each sentence. Then complete the second blank with your own idea.**

| | | |
|---|---|---|
| **create a website** | **install new software** | ~~**write a paragraph**~~ |
| **email a photograph** | **ride a bicycle** | |

1. It's easy to write a paragraph if you follow the four steps in the writing process.
2. It is simple to ______ if you ______.
3. Anyone can learn to ______ if he or she ______.
4. To ______, just ______.
5. You can learn to ______ by ______.

**TRY IT OUT!** Write three topic sentences for "how-to" paragraphs. Use three of the suggestions from the box or think of your own topics. You will use one of these topics to write your own "how-to" paragraph on page 103.

**Topic Suggestions**

- Avoid studying for a test
- Catch a fish
- Change a flat tire
- Check the oil in a car
- Get an A in English
- Get an F in English
- Make a cup of coffee
- Make pizza (or any special food)
- Meet people in a new place
- Prepare for a job interview
- Raise a happy child
- Study for a test
- Train a cat/dog/parrot
- Use chopsticks

*You can clean your room in ten minutes by following these simple steps.*

1. ______________________________

2. ______________________________

3. ______________________________

## TIME-ORDER AND LISTING-ORDER TRANSITION SIGNALS

In a "how-to" paragraph, you can use either **time-order transition signals** or **listing-order transition signals**. Notice in the chart that many time-order and listing-order transition signals are the same.

Keep these rules in mind when you write a "how-to" paragraph:

| Rules | Examples |
|---|---|
| 1. Use time-order transition signals if the steps in your instructions must be in a specific order (such as in the writing model about how to have a successful yard sale). | First, decide on a day and time for your sale.<br>Next, look through your family's belongings and collect used items in good condition. |
| 2. Use listing-order signals if your paragraph contains a number of tips that can be discussed in any order. | First, find out all that you can about the company before the job interview.<br>Second, make a list of all of your strengths and weaknesses, and be prepared to talk about them. |

| Transition Signals | | |
|---|---|---|
| **Time Order** | | **Listing Order** |
| First,<br>First of all,<br>Second,<br>Third,<br>Next,<br>After that,<br>Then<br>Finally, | before a test<br>in the morning<br>during a flight | First,<br>First of all,<br>Second,<br>Third,<br>In addition,<br>Also,<br>Finally, |

Note that most transition signals usually appear at the beginning of a sentence, followed by a comma. *Then* is an exception. Do not put a comma after *then*.

> **Next,** spread out the pizza dough. **Then** cover it with your favorite sauce and toppings.

The phrases in the chart in the second column under Time Order are just a few examples of a wide range of time expressions that you can use as time-order signals. You can put time expressions like these at the beginning of a sentence (usually followed by a comma) or at the end of a sentence. You do not need to add a comma before a time expression at the end of a sentence.

> **Before a big test,** get a good night's sleep.
>
> Get a good night's sleep **before a big test.**
>
> **In the morning,** be sure to eat breakfast.
>
> Be sure to eat breakfast **in the morning.**

**Writing Tip**

It is not necessary to put a transition signal at the beginning of every sentence in a "how-to" paragraph. A paragraph with too many transition signals is just as confusing to the reader as a paragraph with none!

**PRACTICE 4** **Time Order or Listing Order?**

Work in pairs or a small group. Decide whether each topic requires time order or listing order. Write *TO* for time order and *LO* for listing order.

______ 1. How to study for a test

______ 2. How to get in shape

______ 3. How to change the oil in a car

______ 4. How to meet people in a new place

______ 5. How to impress your boss

______ 6. How to learn a new language

______ 7. How to clean a computer keyboard

______ 8. How to write a paragraph

______ 9. How to get a driver's license

______ 10. How to prepare for an earthquake

**PRACTICE 5** **Organizing "How-To" Paragraphs**

**A** Number the sentences in each group to show the correct order. Note that three of the sentence groups require time order and one group requires listing order.

**GROUP 1**

**How to Prevent Jet Lag[1]**

______ Don't drink coffee or energy drinks during the flight.

______ On your first night, try to go to bed at your normal hour in your new time zone.

______ Eat a high-carbohydrate meal[2] before your flight.

______ On the day you arrive, don't nap[3] during the day.

______ Frequent flyers recommend these steps to prevent jet lag.

[1] **jet lag:** feeling of being very tired after traveling a long distance in an airplane

[2] **high-carbohydrate meal:** a meal that includes foods such as rice, pasta, potatoes, and breads

[3] **nap:** sleep for a short time

## Group 2

### How to Drive Your Teacher Crazy

3 Yawn and check your cell phone as often as possible during the class.

2 Make a lot of noise when you enter the classroom.

5 It's easy to drive your teacher crazy if you follow these simple directions.

4 At least five minutes before the end of class, slam your books shut and stare at the door.

1 Always come to class at least five minutes late.

## Group 3

### How to Plan a Family Vacation

2 Consider the interests and abilities of everyone in the family.

3 Decide how long you can be away from home.

4 Decide how much money you can spend.

1 Planning a family vacation takes careful thought.

5 Find out when everyone can take time off from school and jobs.

6 When you have thought about all these things, you are ready to visit a travel agency or begin researching your vacation online.

*(continued on next page)*

**Group 4**

### How to Write a Book Report

2 Choose an interesting book, and make a schedule for reading.

4 Before you begin, however, reread the assignment and your instructor's directions.

5 Start reading your book.

9 Read your book report assignment carefully, and make sure you follow the directions.

6 As you read, take notes about the characters and what happens to them.

1 To write a good book report, follow these simple steps.

3 Calculate how many pages per day you need to read and schedule several days to write your report.

7 Make an outline, write your first draft, and then edit your report.

8 You may want to write down a few quotes to use later in your report.

10 After you finish reading, it's time to write your report.

**B** **Choose two groups from Part A and rewrite them as "how-to" paragraphs on a separate sheet of paper. Follow these steps for each paragraph:**

- First, copy the title and topic sentence.
- Next, copy the remaining sentences in order.
- Then add transition signals where needed.
- Finally, add a concluding sentence. (For ideas, look back at the examples on page 77.)

*How to Prevent Jet Lag*

*Frequent flyers recommend these steps to prevent jet lag.*

*First of all, eat a high-carbohydrate meal before your flight. . . .*

## OUTLINING

In Chapter 2, you practiced using outlining to organize the ideas you got from clustering. In this section, you will practice using outlining to organize the ideas you get from listing.

In order to go from a list to an outline, there is another step you must perform: editing your list. To understand the process better, let's look at the steps the writer of the writing model on page 74 used to go from listing to outlining.

### STEP 1: Use listing to get ideas.

First, the writer used the listing technique to get his ideas. Here is the list he started with:

How to Have a Successful Yard Sale

| | |
|---|---|
| look through belongings and collect used things in good condition | people don't buy broken or dirty things |
| —clothes | get change from bank |
| —toys | ask your friends to help |
| —books | decide on the prices |
| —old dishes, etc. | put a price tag on each item |
| store them in the garage | buy price tags |
| clean everything | make sure everything is clean |
| clean the garage | wash and iron the clothes |
| arrange items on tables | advertise |
| borrow tables | try to have sale on a sunny day |
| make signs | decide on a day and time |
| put signs around the neighborhood | be prepared to bargain |
| | get up early |

### STEP 2: Edit the list.

The writer's second step was to edit the list. He did this in two stages:

- First, he read through the list and crossed out repeated ideas and information that he felt was unimportant.
- Next, he decided what the main steps were, and then he numbered them using time order.

Here is what his edited list looked like:

How to Have a Successful Yard Sale

2 look through belongings and collect used things in good condition
—clothes
—toys
—books
—old dishes, etc.
6 store them in the garage
3 clean everything
~~clean the garage~~
11 arrange items on tables
~~borrow tables~~
8 make signs
9 put signs around the neighborhood

~~people don't buy broken or dirty things~~
7 get change from bank
ask your friends to help
4 decide on the prices
5 put a price tag on each item
~~buy price tags~~
~~make sure everything is clean~~
~~wash and iron the clothes~~
~~advertise~~
~~try to have sale on a sunny day~~
1 decide on a day and time
~~be prepared to bargain~~
10 get up early

### STEP 3: Create the outline.

The writer's next step was to make an outline from the edited list. To do this, he used a new sheet of paper and wrote down his title and his main points so he could see them clearly. Notice that he changed the numbers to capital letters (A, B, C, D, and so on). As he did this, he also took the opportunity to combine some of the steps on his list that were closely related (see steps D, G, and H). Finally, he added a topic sentence at the beginning and a concluding sentence at the end.

Here is his completed outline:

| | |
|---|---|
| TITLE | How to Have a Successful Yard Sale |
| TOPIC SENTENCE | In order to have a successful yard sale, you need to prepare well by following these simple steps. |
| MAIN POINTS | A. Decide on a day and time.<br>B. Look through belongings and collect used items in good condition.<br>C. Clean the items.<br>D. Decide on the prices and mark a price on each item.<br>E. Store the items in the garage.<br>F. Get change from a bank.<br>G. Make signs and put them around the neighborhood.<br>H. Get up early and arrange items on tables in your driveway or yard. |
| CONCLUDING SENTENCE | If you follow all of these steps, your yard sale will be a great success. |

**PRACTICE 6** **Creating an Outline**

**Use the list you made in Practice 1 on pages 72–73 to make an outline. Follow the directions.**

**1.** Edit your list.

- Edit the list by crossing out repeated ideas or ideas that you don't think are important.
- Decide whether to use time order or listing order.
- If you use time order, identify the main steps and number them in order. If you use listing order, number the points in the order you want to discuss them.

**2.** Create the outline.

- On a separate piece of paper, write down your title and leave the next 2–3 lines blank. (These are for the topic sentence that you will add at the end.)
- Consider the numbered steps or tips in your edited list to see if there are any that you can combine.
- Write your main points in order and label them *A, B, C,* and so on.
- Add a topic sentence under the title and a concluding sentence at the end.

**TRY IT OUT!** On a separate sheet of paper, write a paragraph using the outline you created in Practice 6. Follow these directions:

1. Follow your outline as you write your draft.
2. Use transition signals to introduce the most important steps.
3. If you wish, add other sentences to explain each step in more detail.
4. Review the words in Looking at Vocabulary (on pages 75–76). Consider adding these or other adverbs of manner to make it clear how you want your readers to perform the actions you describe.
5. Proofread your paragraph and correct any mistakes.

## SENTENCE STRUCTURE

In Chapters 1 and 2, you learned about simple and compound sentences. A third kind of sentence is a **complex sentence**. Before we look at this sentence type, it's important to understand some basic concepts about clauses.

### INDEPENDENT AND DEPENDENT CLAUSES

A **clause** is a group of words that contains a subject and a verb. There are two kinds of clauses in English: **independent clauses** and **dependent clauses**.

An **independent clause** is a group of words that has a subject and a verb and expresses a complete thought. It can stand alone as a sentence by itself.

S V
Paris has excellent art museums.

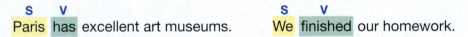

S V
We finished our homework.

A **dependent clause** is also a group of words that has a subject and a verb. Unlike an independent clause, however, a dependent clause always begins with an introductory word known as a **subordinator**.

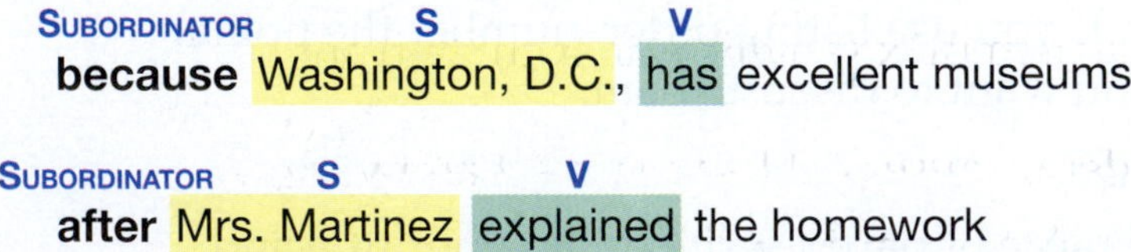


A dependent clause does not express a complete thought. It is not a complete sentence, so it cannot stand alone. To be correct, it must appear in a sentence with an independent clause. Together, the two clauses express a complete thought and form a complex sentence.

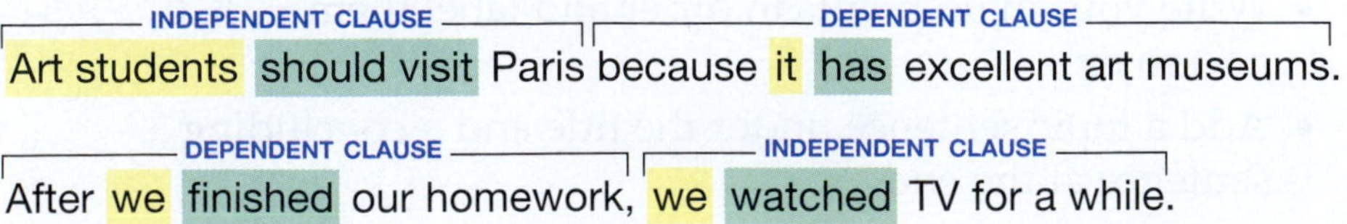

**PRACTICE 7** **Identifying Independent and Dependent Clauses**

**Look at each group of words from a student paragraph. If it is an independent clause, write *IC* and put a period at the end. If it is a dependent clause, write *DC* and circle the subordinator.**

DC 1. Before I go to work

IC 2. I take a walk around the block.

IC 3. The exercise wakes up my body and clears my mind

IC 4. It's hard to do this in the winter

DC 5. When I go to work

IC 6. It is still dark

DC 7. After I get home from work

IC 8. It is dark again

IC 9. I can always take a walk on weekends, even in the winter

DC 10. When it is raining, of course

IC 11. I never go out

DC 12. On rainy days, as soon as the alarm clock rings

IC 13. I turn over and go back to sleep

## COMPLEX SENTENCES WITH TIME CLAUSES

A **complex sentence** has one independent clause and one (or more) dependent clauses. In this chapter, you will explore complex sentences with time clauses. In Chapter 5, you will look at complex sentences with clauses of reason and condition; and in Chapter 6, you will look at complex sentences with adjective clauses.

### Complex Sentences with Time Clauses

In this section, you will look at complex sentences that contain an independent clause and a special kind of dependent clause known as a **time clause**. A time clause is a dependent clause that has a subject and verb and begins with an introductory word known as a **time subordinator**. Time clauses are easy to identify because they answer the question *When?*

INDEPENDENT CLAUSE — DEPENDENT TIME CLAUSE

Anna's family eats dinner **as soon as** her father comes home.

(Anna's family = S, eats = V; as soon as = TIME SUBORDINATOR; her father = S, comes = V)

Here are examples of common time subordinators and how you can use them in complex sentences:

| Time Subordinators | |
|---|---|
| **after** | I will go straight to bed after I finish writing this paragraph. |
| **as soon as** | She felt better as soon as she took the medicine. |
| **before** | Wait for a green light before you cross a street. |
| **since** | It has been a year since I left home. |
| **until** | We can't leave the room until everyone finishes the test. |
| **when** | Where were you when I called? |
| **whenever** | Whenever I don't sleep well, I feel sick the next day. |
| **while** | My neighbors were having a party while I was trying to sleep. |

Note that in complex sentences with time clauses, the independent and dependent clauses can be in any order.

- If the independent clause comes first, don't use a comma.

NO COMMA

INDEPENDENT — DEPENDENT

We ran for shelter as soon as it started to rain.

- If the dependent clause comes first, put a comma after it.

COMMA

DEPENDENT — INDEPENDENT

As soon as it started to rain, we ran for shelter.

**PRACTICE 8** **Analyzing Complex Sentences with Time Clauses**

**Underline each independent clause once and each dependent clause twice. Circle each time subordinator and add a comma as needed.**

1. After we won the lottery last year, my wife and I immediately decided to take a trip.
2. We were very excited when we won.
3. After we got our first payment we started planning a trip to Italy.
4. Before we left on our trip we wrote to our cousins in Rome and told them our plans.
5. As soon as they received our letter they called and invited us to stay with them.

6. They were waiting at the airport when we arrived.

7. They waited outside while the Italian officials carefully checked our passports and luggage.

8. Finally, after we got our suitcases, they drove us to their home.

9. As soon as we arrived at their apartment they wanted to feed us.

10. We ate one delicious home-cooked dish after another until we were very full.

11. We fell asleep as soon as our heads hit the pillows.

12. Almost 24 hours had passed since we left home.

## PRACTICE 9 Writing Complex Sentences with Time Clauses

**A** Look at Practice 7 on page 87. Write complex sentences with time clauses by combining the word groups shown. Add commas as needed.

1. **Combine 1 and 2:** Before I go to work, I take a walk around the block.

2. **Combine 5 and 6:** ______________________

3. **Combine 7 and 8:** ______________________

4. **Combine 10 and 11:** ______________________

5. **Combine 12 and 13:** ______________________

**B** Read each clause in column A. Find the clause in column B that completes it, and write the letter of the clause on the line. (HINT: When completed, the sentences tell a continuous story.)

**A**

1. The trip began badly b
2. It was almost noon g
3. As soon as I threw out my fishing line f
4. I spent most of the afternoon untangling[1] my line e
5. After we had been fishing for a couple of hours h
6. We were totally wet a
7. When we got back home d
8. It will be a long, long time c

**B**

a. before we could put on our rain jackets.
b. when we had a flat tire on the way to the lake.
c. until I go fishing with my brothers again.
d. I immediately took a hot shower.
e. while my brothers were catching fish after fish.
f. it got caught in some underwater weeds.
g. before we started fishing.
h. it started to rain.

**C** Write the sentences from Part B in paragraph format. Add commas as needed.

A Miserable Fishing Trip

The trip began badly when we had a flat tire on the way to the lake.

It was almost noon before we started fishing.

As soon as I threw out my fishing line it got caught in some underwater weeds.

I spent most of the afternoon untangling my line while my brothers were catching fish after fish. After we had been fishing for a couple of hours it started to rain We were totally wet before we could put on our rain jacket. When we got back home I immediately took a hot shower. It will be a long, long time until I go fishing with my brothers again.

[1] **untangling:** making straight by removing knots

## COMMON SENTENCE ERRORS: FRAGMENTS

In Chapter 2, you learned about the sentence errors called run-ons and comma splices. Another kind of sentence error is called a **fragment**. The word *fragment* means a part of something. A sentence fragment is only part of a sentence. It is not a complete sentence. These are examples of fragments:

INCORRECT: Before the test began.

INCORRECT: As soon as you get home.

Why are they fragments? Because they are dependent clauses, and as we learned on page 86, a dependent clause is not a complete sentence. Therefore it cannot stand alone.

To fix the error, you have to add an independent clause either before or after the fragment. If you add the independent clause after the fragment, remember to change the period to a comma.

CORRECT: *The teacher passed out paper* before the test began.

OR

Before the test began, *the teacher passed out paper.*

CORRECT: *Call me* as soon as you get home.

OR

As soon as you get home, *call me.*

**PRACTICE 10** **Identifying and Correcting Fragments**

**A** **Read the groups of words. Decide if they are fragments or sentences. Write *F* for fragment and *S* for sentence.**

F 1. Before I learned to speak English well.

S 2. He left Mexico when he was a baby.

_____ 3. Every night, after I finish my homework.

_____ 4. As soon as we heard the crash.

_____ 5. The bicycle racers stopped to rest before they started up the mountain.

_____ 6. Wait until you hear the bell.

_____ 7. Whenever my children have a school holiday.

_____ 8. I work at night while my husband stays home with the children.

**B** Correct each fragment from Part A by adding an independent clause. Write your new sentences on the lines.

1. Before I learned to speak English well, I was afraid to use the telephone.

______

______

______

## SUMMARY: SIMPLE, COMPOUND, AND COMPLEX SENTENCES

Good writers add interest and variety to their writing by using a mixture of simple, compound, and complex sentences. Here is a summary of what you have learned about these sentence types so far.

| SENTENCE TYPE | EXAMPLES |
|---|---|
| 1. A **simple sentence** has one independent clause. | It was a sunny day.<br>Raise your hand to ask a question. |
| 2. A **compound sentence** has two or more independent clauses joined by a comma and a coordinating conjunction. | It was a sunny day, so we went to the beach.<br>Talk quietly, or don't talk at all. |
| 3. A **complex sentence** has one independent and one or more dependent clauses. In complex sentences with time clauses, a comma is needed when the dependent time clause comes before the independent clause. | While the meat is cooking, prepare the sauce.<br>Prepare the sauce while the meat is cooking. |

**PRACTICE 11** **Identifying Simple, Compound, and Complex Sentences**

**A** Analyze the sentences. Underline each independent clause once and each dependent clause twice. Then write *simple*, *compound*, or *complex* on the line at the right.

**SENTENCE TYPE**

1. Some people like to relax and do nothing when they take a vacation. complex
2. Other people like to travel, and still others like to have an adventure. ______
3. Unusual vacations are becoming popular. ______

4. For example, people go hiking in Nepal or river rafting in Ecuador. ________

5. Some people spend their vacations learning, and some spend their vacations helping others. ________

6. A friend of mine likes to help people, so he spent his summer helping to build a school in Bangladesh. ________

7. After he returned home, he wanted to go back to help build a medical clinic. ________

8. People may find life at home a little boring after they have climbed volcanoes or ridden camels. ________

**B** **Read the paragraph. Then use the sentence numbers to complete the sentence analysis.**

### How to Succeed in a U.S. College

1 Succeeding in a U.S. college may require new strategies for students from other cultures. 2 I survived my first year of college in the United States, so I feel qualified to suggest a few tips about colleges here. 3 First, attend every class. 4 Professors talk about the most important material in class. 5 When you aren't there, you miss important information. 6 Second, take good notes. 7 Then review or recopy your notes as soon as you can. 8 Third, don't be afraid to ask questions whenever you don't understand something. 9 Professors want their students to succeed, so they want them to ask questions. 10 Fourth, get to know your professors personally. 11 Go to their office during office hours, and introduce yourself. 12 Finally, get involved in a campus activity, or get a job in the bookstore. 13 Go to football and basketball games, and join a club. 14 Be friendly, and talk to everyone—other students, professors, secretaries, cafeteria workers, and janitors. 15 Active, involved students are successful students.

**Sentence Analysis**

Simple: __1__ ______ ______ ______ ______ ______

Compound: ______ ______ ______ ______ ______ ______

Complex: ______ ______ ______

**PRACTICE 12** Combining Details

**A** Discuss the meaning of the words in the box. Then use the nouns marked with an asterisk (*) to label the images.

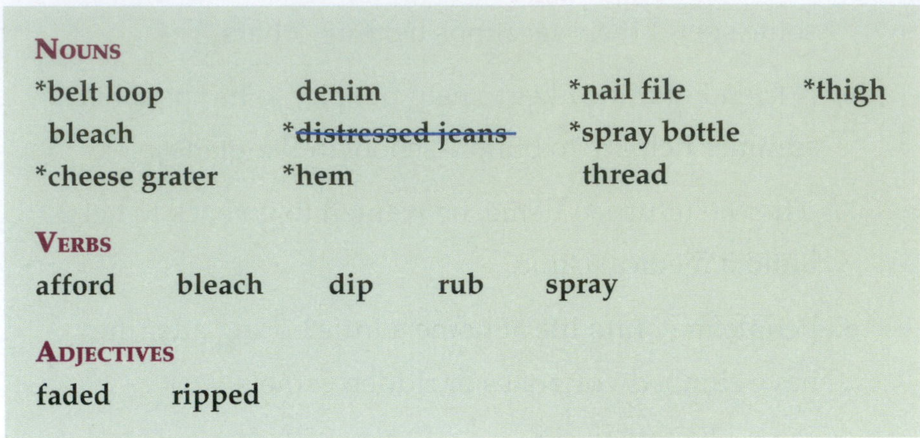

**NOUNS**

*belt loop, denim, *nail file, *thigh, bleach, *~~distressed jeans~~, *spray bottle, *cheese grater, *hem, thread

**VERBS**

afford, bleach, dip, rub, spray

**ADJECTIVES**

faded, ripped

1. distressed jeans

a. ______________

b. ______________

c. ______________

2. ______________ 3. ______________ 4. ______________

**B** On a separate sheet of paper, combine the sentences in each group to make a simple, compound, or complex sentence. For some, there may be more than one answer.

### How to Make Your Own Distressed[1] Jeans

1. a. Would you like to own a pair of distressed jeans?

   b. You can't afford to pay designer prices.

   *1. Would you like to own a pair of distressed jeans but can't afford to pay designer prices?*

2. a. Follow these instructions to make your own pair of jeans.

   b. The jeans are stylishly ripped.

   c. The jeans are stylishly faded.

3. a. Buy a pair of inexpensive new jeans.

   b. Use a pair that you already own.

4. a. Find the direction of the lines in the denim fabric.

   b. Rub a knife back and forth over the lines.

5. a. You can also use a cheese grater.

   b. You can also use a nail file.

6. a. Keep rubbing.

   b. White threads appear. (Hint: Use *until*.)

7. a. You want the white threads to stay there.

   b. Don't cut them. (Hint: Use *so*.)

8. a. Dip an old toothbrush into bleach.

   b. Run the old toothbrush around the edges of the back pockets.

   c. Run the old toothbrush over the belt loops.

9. a. Mix a little bleach with water in a spray bottle.

   b. Spray the thighs and seat of the jeans.

10. a. Wash and dry the jeans several times. (Hint: Use *after you*.)

    b. Your new jeans will look stylishly old!

---

[1] **distressed:** (of fabric) made or processed to look faded and worn-out as if by age or hard use

**C** On a separate sheet of paper, write the ten sentences in Part B as a "how-to" paragraph. Add time-order transition signals as needed before the main steps.

*How to Make Your Own Distressed Jeans*

*Would you like to own a pair of designer jeans but can't afford to pay designer prices? Follow these instructions to . . . . First of all, . . .*

## MECHANICS

### CAPITALIZATION: FOUR MORE RULES

In Chapter 1, you learned six rules for capitalizing words in English (see pages 18–19). Here are four additional rules:

| RULES | EXAMPLES | |
|---|---|---|
| **Capitalize:** | | |
| **1.** names of specific structures such as buildings, roads, and bridges | the White House<br>the Hilton Hotel<br>the Kremlin | Highway 395<br>State Route 15<br>the Brooklyn Bridge |
| **2.** names of specific organizations, such as businesses, schools, and clubs | American Express<br>Stanford University | the United Nations<br>Outdoor Club |
| **3.** names of the days, months, holidays, and special time periods | Monday<br>January | New Year's Day<br>Ramadan |
| BUT NOT: the names of seasons | spring<br>summer | fall (autumn)<br>winter |
| **4.** geographic areas | the Middle East<br>Southeast Asia | the Southwest<br>Eastern Europe |
| BUT NOT: compass directions | Drive south for a mile and turn west. | |

## PRACTICE 13 Using Capitalization

Work with a partner or a group. Write your own examples of Rules 1–4.

**RULE 1**

**a.** a building: ______________________________

______________________________

**b.** a road: ______________________________

______________________________

**c.** a bridge: ______________________________

______________________________

**RULE 2**

**a.** a business: ______________________________

______________________________

**b.** a club: ______________________________

______________________________

**c.** a school: ______________________________

______________________________

**RULE 3**

**a.** a day: ______________________________

______________________________

**b.** a month: ______________________________

______________________________

**c.** a holiday: ______________________________

______________________________

**RULE 4**

**a.** a geographic area in your country: ______________________________

______________________________

**b.** elsewhere in the world: ______________________________

______________________________

## PRACTICE 14 Editing Capitalization Errors

Work alone or with a partner. Read the email. Change the small letters to capital letters where necessary.

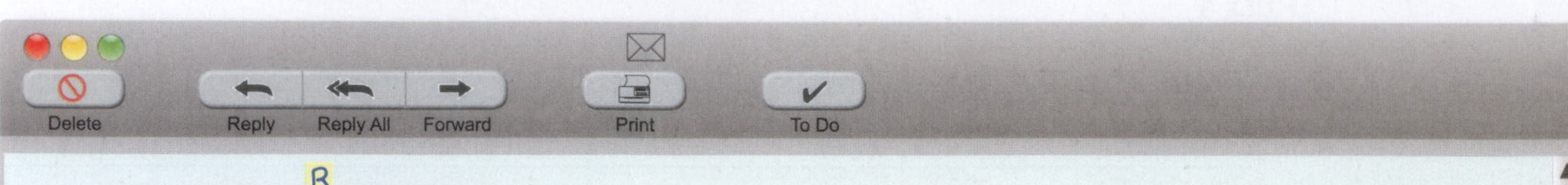


**From:** Heather richmond
**To:** Stacie Gomez
**Subject:** Trip

---

dear stacie,

I am so happy that you are coming to visit me this summer. I hope that you will be able to stay until july 4th. We are planning a big picnic on that day to celebrate independence day here in the united states.

You asked for directions to my house from the airport, so here they are. The Internet or a GPS device will give you several different routes, but this is the best one. From the airport, go north on U.s. 101, and then go west on 380. Take 380 to 280, going north. From 280, merge onto route 1. route 1 is also called 19th avenue. You will pass san francisco state university and a large shopping center. Continue on 19th avenue through golden gate park. Soon you will come to the famous golden gate bridge. Drive across the bridge, and continue north for about 10 more miles. You will pass the towns of sausalito, mill valley, and larkspur. In larkspur, take the exit for sir francis drake boulevard from the highway.

Drive west for three blocks, and then turn left onto elm avenue. Finally, go one block down elm and turn right. My apartment is in the marina towers. The address is 155 west hillside drive.

Be sure to bring warm clothes because it is cool in june and july in this part of california. I can't wait to see you!

Love,

Heather

## PUNCTUATION: COMMAS

There are many rules for using commas. You have already learned the first three. Rule 4 is new.

| RULES | EXAMPLES |
|---|---|
| **Use a comma:** | |
| **1.** after listing-order and time-order signals | First, put four cups of rice into a pan.<br>After that, fold the paper in half again.<br>After the test, go out and celebrate. |
| EXCEPTION: *then* | Then turn left onto Oak Street. |
| **2.** before coordinating conjunctions in a compound sentence | Some people like to travel, and others like to have an adventure.<br>Cook the steak over high heat for six minutes, but don't let it burn. |
| EXCEPTION: Sometimes writers omit this comma in very short sentences. | Dogs bark and cats meow.<br>Turn left and drive one block. |
| **3.** in a complex sentence, when a dependent time clause comes before an independent clause | While you are waiting for the pizza dough to rise, make the sauce.<br>After you take the pizza out of the oven, cut it into eight pieces. |
| **4.** to separate items in a series<br>(A series is three or more related things, people, or actions that occur one after the other.) | One dog, one cat, two goldfish, a bird, and four humans live at our house.<br>John, Mary, and I are classmates.<br>Every morning I get up early, run a mile, take a shower, eat breakfast, and feed my pets.<br>Turn left at the stoplight, go one block, and turn right. |

**PRACTICE 15** **Editing for Commas**

 Work alone or with a partner. Find the eight comma mistakes in Paragraph 1 and the 10 comma mistakes in Paragraph 2. Make corrections.

**Paragraph 1**

### How to Choose Your College Courses

There are many things to consider before you register for college courses. First make a list of the required courses that you must take and then put a checkmark by the courses that you should take in this academic year. If you have questions about required courses ask your advisor your instructor or a classmate. Then think about your course load. How many courses can you take? Which courses will require the most study time? Choose a variety of courses and levels of difficulty. Finally check the times the days and the instructors for each course. After you make your final choices you'll be ready to register.

**Paragraph 2**

### How to Fail a Driving Test

It's easy to fail a driving test if you really try hard. First park your car with your two right wheels far up on the curb. When you do that your instructor will have trouble getting into the car. Second pull away from the curb really fast and don't look in the mirror or signal. After that drive your car into a road sign or a parked car. Don't stop at stop signs and speed up to get through intersections quickly. Then try to make your tires squeal loudly while you are turning corners. Next look for an opportunity to turn the wrong way down a one-way street. Finally don't stop for pedestrians in crosswalks and use your horn to frighten them out of your way. Just one of these techniques will probably get you an F on your driving test and two or more certainly will.

**B** Answer the questions. Use the instructions in parentheses and the sentence beginnings provided. Remember to separate three or more items in a series with commas.

1. What three foods do you like the most? (Use *and* before the last item.)

   I like Japanese sushi, Middle Eastern falafel, and Mexican tacos.

2. What three foods don't you like? (Use *or* before the last item.)

   I don't like ______________________________.

3. What are three places you might go on your honeymoon? (Use *or* before the last item.)

   On my honeymoon, I might go to ______________________________

   ______________________________.

4. What are six useful items you should always take on a hike? (Use *and* before the last item.)

   Whenever you go on a hike, be sure to take ______________________________

   ______________________________.

5. What are two animals that don't get along with each other? (Use *and*.)

   ______________________________ don't get along with each other.

6. What are three things you do every morning? (Use *and*.)

   Every morning, I ______________________________

   ______________________________.

7. What are two things you always do and one thing you never do on weekends? (Use both *and* and *but*. Write a compound sentence.)

   On weekends, I always ______________________________

   ______________________________.

8. What are three kinds of TV shows that you enjoy watching and two kinds that you dislike watching? (Use both *and* and *but*. Write a compound sentence.)

   I enjoy watching ______________________________

   ______________________________.

## Applying Vocabulary: Using Descriptive Adverbs

Before you begin your writing assignment, review what you learned about words that describe how to do things on pages 75–76.

**PRACTICE 16** **Using Words that Describe How to Do Things**

**Use each phrase to write a sentence about a person you know. Then use a word from the box to write a second sentence that gives an example or adds more information.**

| attractively | cheaply | easily | thoroughly |
|---|---|---|---|
| carefully | clearly | hard | well |

**1.** dresses attractively

*My aunt always dresses attractively. Her closet is full of clothes, so she can choose her outfits carefully.*

**2.** doesn't speak clearly

______________________________

______________________________

**3.** studies very hard

______________________________

______________________________

**4.** plays a sport well

______________________________

______________________________

**5.** learns languages easily

______________________________

______________________________

**6.** treats animals gently

______________________________

______________________________

## WRITING ASSIGNMENT

Your writing assignment for this chapter is to write a "how-to" paragraph using a topic from the Try It Out! activity on page 78. Organize your ideas by using time order or listing order. Follow the steps in the writing process.

Prewrite

### STEP 1: Prewrite to get ideas.

- Use listing to get ideas. Follow the procedure on pages 71 and 83.
- When you are done, edit your list by crossing out any unimportant or repeated information.
- Decide whether you will use time order or listing order. Then number the steps or tips.
- Make an outline. Use the procedure and format on pages 84–85. Your outline should include a title, a topic sentence, main points, and a concluding sentence.
- Review the words in Looking at Vocabulary and Applying Vocabulary on pages 75–76 and 102. Look at your outline again and, if possible, add in some of these (or similar) words.

### STEP 2: Write the first draft.

- Write *FIRST DRAFT* at the top of your paper.
- Follow your outline to write your paragraph.
- Add time-order or listing-order transition signals to the main steps or tips.
- Try to include at least three complex sentences.

### STEP 3: Revise and edit the first draft.

- Exchange papers with a partner and give each other feedback. Use Chapter 3 Peer Review on page 210.
- Consider your partner's feedback and revise your paragraph. Mark changes on your first draft.
- Check your work against the Chapter 3 Writer's Self-Check on page 211, and make more changes as needed.

### STEP 4: Write a new draft.

- Refer to the changes you made on your first draft and do a final draft of your paragraph.
- Proofread it carefully.
- Hand it in to your teacher. Your teacher may also ask you to hand in your prewriting, your outline, and your first draft.

## SELF-ASSESSMENT

In this chapter, you learned to:

- ❍ Use listing to get ideas for writing
- ❍ Organize a "how-to" paragraph using time order or listing order
- ❍ Edit a list of ideas to create an outline
- ❍ Work with complex sentences with time clauses
- ❍ Correct sentence fragments
- ❍ Use additional rules for capitalization and commas
- ❍ Write, revise, and edit a "how-to" paragraph

Which ones can you do well? Mark them ✓

Which ones do you need to practice more? Mark them ✗

# EXPANSION

## TIMED WRITING

To succeed in academic writing you need to be able to write quickly and fluently. For example, you might have to write a paragraph for a test in class, and you only have 30 minutes. In this activity, you will write a paragraph in class. You will have 30 minutes. To complete the activity in time, follow the directions.

1. Read the prompt below (or the prompt your teacher assigns) carefully. Make sure you understand the question or task. Then decide on the topic of your paragraph. (3 minutes)
2. Use listing to get ideas. Then read over your list and decide which ideas you will write about. Edit your list and then make an outline to organize your ideas. (5 minutes)
3. Write your paragraph. Be sure to include a title, a topic sentence, time-order or listing-order transition signals, supporting ideas, and a concluding sentence. (15 minutes)
4. Proofread your paragraph. Correct any mistakes. (7 minutes)
5. Give your paper to your teacher.

**Prompt:** Write a paragraph describing how to do well in a certain class. You can write about a class you are taking now or a class you took in the past. Imagine that you are giving advice to a new student.

## YOUR JOURNAL

Continue making entries in your journal. If you cannot think of a topic for a journal entry, try one of these ideas:

- Do you remember learning how to do something special from a family member? Perhaps your parent or grandparent taught you how to do something when you were young. Describe what happened and what you learned.
- Do you have a special hobby or talent? For example, do you play the violin, or do you collect something? Explain how to do something. For example, you can explain how to tune a violin or how to find good bargains online.
- What do you know how to repair? Can you sew on a button, fix a leaking faucet, or replace the ink cartridge in your printer? Explain how to repair something.

*For more ideas for journal entries, see Appendix A on page 193.*

CHAPTER 4

# DESCRIBING WITH SPACE ORDER

## OBJECTIVES

**Writers need certain skills.**

**In this chapter, you will learn to:**

- Use listing to get ideas for describing a place
- Organize a descriptive paragraph using space order
- Develop a description with specific details
- Identify adjectives and use them in the correct order
- Vary the structure of sentences with prepositional phrases
- Write, revise, and edit a descriptive paragraph

*Writing a description is like painting a picture. What words can you use to describe the place in the artist's painting?*

## INTRODUCTION

In this chapter, you will learn how to organize information in a descriptive paragraph using space order. You will also learn about using adjectives and prepositional phrases to help you add detail to your writing.

To help you get ideas for your paragraphs, you will first do some prewriting.

## PREWRITING

In Chapter 3, you used listing as a prewriting technique to brainstorm ideas for "how-to" paragraphs. In this chapter, you will see how listing can be used to brainstorm ideas for descriptive paragraphs.

### LISTING DESCRIPTIVE DETAILS

Descriptions are like "word pictures." They give readers a mental picture of how something looks, feels, tastes, and sounds. To write a good description, you need to become a sharp observer and notice many small details. A good way to start is to think about the place, object, or person you want to describe. Then make a list of all the words and phrases that come into your mind. As you do so, you can also think of ways to describe where things are by using phrases beginning with prepositions such as *on, in, under,* and *on top of.*

**PRACTICE 1** Using Listing to Get Ideas

**A** Work with a partner. Is the meaning of each adjective positive or negative? Write + for positive and – for negative.

**ADJECTIVES THAT DESCRIBE A PERSON**

| | | | |
|---|---|---|---|
| + athletic | careful | hardworking | neat |
| boring | disorganized | lazy | messy |

**ADJECTIVES THAT DESCRIBE A PLACE**

| | | | |
|---|---|---|---|
| clean | dark | small | sunny |
| cluttered | messy | spacious | tidy |

**B** Look at pictures 1 and 2 on pages 108–109. What kind of person do you think lives or works in each place? What general impression does each room create? Use the words from Part A to fill in the first two lines under each picture.

**C** With a partner, look at the words above pictures 1 and 2. Locate the nouns in each picture. Then use the words in the boxes to list as many details as you can. Save your lists to use in the Try It Out! activity on page 120.

### PICTURE 1: Bedroom in College Dormitory

**Nouns**

| | | | | |
|---|---|---|---|---|
| bed | comforter | curtain | laptop | speakers |
| bookshelves | corkboard | lamp | pillows | whiteboard |

**Prepositions**

in front of | next to | on the left/right | to the left/right of | under

Kind of person who lives here: messy, ____________

General impression of room: ____________

Details:

bed next to the window

comforter, pillows on unmade bed

## PICTURE 2: Instructor's Office

**Nouns**

| | | | | |
|---|---|---|---|---|
| armchairs | desk | diplomas | nameplate | pitcher |
| bookcase | desk chair | figurine | pen set | portrait |
| cabinet | desk pad | lamp | photos | rug |

**Prepositions**

against behind in front of next to on the left/right under

**Kind of person who works here:** organized, ____________________

**General impression of room:** ____________________

**Details:**

____________________ ____________________

____________________ ____________________

____________________ ____________________

____________________ ____________________

____________________ ____________________

____________________ ____________________

____________________ ____________________

____________________ ____________________

## DESCRIPTIVE PARAGRAPHS

There are two keys to writing a good description:

- Using space order to organize your ideas
- Using supporting sentences with specific detail to help your reader visualize what you are describing.

In the next section, you'll learn about different kinds of space order.

### SPACE ORDER

Imagine that you are standing in the doorway of your classroom. How would you describe the room to someone who has never seen it? In what order would you describe the things you see? Here are some possibilities:

- **Clockwise:** You might start your description at the doorway and work your way around the room in a clockwise direction until you reach the doorway again.
- **Front to back:** You might start your description at the front of the room and go from front to back, first describing the chalkboard or whiteboard, the teacher's desk, and the area around the teacher's desk. Then you might describe the students' desks in the center of the room, and finally the walls and/or windows at the back and sides of the room.

These two ways of organizing a description are common types of **space order**. When your description moves through a space in a clear direction, it helps your reader imagine what you are describing. Other possibilities include:

| | | | |
|---|---|---|---|
| top to bottom | far to near | right to left | outside to inside |
| bottom to top | near to far | left to right | inside to outside |

Writers often use space order to describe a place (for example, a room, a building, or even a city), but they can also use it to describe an object (such as a car or a cell phone) or even a person.

## LOOKING AT THE MODEL

The writing model describes a lecture hall at a community college. As you read, notice how the writer carefully moves his focus from one location to another around the room.

**Work with a partner or in a small group. Read the model. Then answer the questions.**

### Writing Model

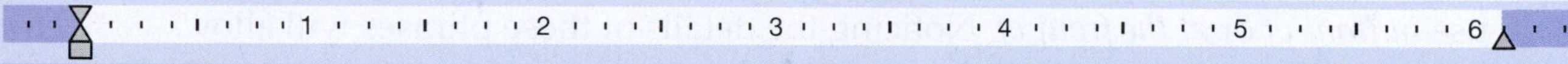

**The New Lecture Hall**

Our community college's beautiful new lecture hall is spacious, modern, and comfortable. On the front wall, there is a large white screen. Instructors can use this for projecting overhead transparencies, slide shows, and audiovisual presentations. Behind the screen, there is a huge whiteboard. To the left of the screen is a clock, and underneath the clock are the light switches. There are two black leather armchairs against the wall. At the front of the lecture hall is the instructor's desk. It's very modern and curved, and it's made of beautiful wood. It looks elegant, in fact. In the center of the desk, there is an overhead projector, and next to it is a computer. To the right of the desk is a lectern. Some instructors like to stand at the lectern and talk. In the main part of the lecture hall, in front of the teacher's desk, there are about 30 rows of seats for students. The black seats are cushioned, so they are comfortable to sit on during long lectures. On the left of each seat, there is a small folding tabletop. Students can use these when they want something to write on. There's also 3 feet of space between the rows, so students have room to stretch their legs. To sum up, our new lecture hall is a pleasing and comfortable place to learn.

### Questions about the Model

1. Does the topic sentence create a positive or negative impression of the lecture hall?
2. Which space order does the writer use to describe the lecture hall: clockwise, front to back, back to front, or top to bottom?
3. The writer describes three main areas of the lecture hall. What are they?

## Looking at Vocabulary: Prepositions of Place

When you write a description of a place, you will often use words and phrases starting with prepositions to describe where things are.

> **In the back of the room** is a large white cabinet. There's a clock **above the cabinet.**

You may already know the meaning of many prepositions, but a challenge that all learners face is to use them accurately. For example, it's easy to confuse *in*, *on*, and *at*. It's also common for learners to have trouble knowing whether to use *in front of* or *at the front of*. Noticing the details of these phrases will allow you to use them more accurately.

### PRACTICE 2 Looking at Prepositions of Place

**A** **Look at objects 1–10. Circle the first mention of each of these in the writing model on page 111, and underline the phrase that describes where it is. Then use the underlined words to complete phrases in the second column.**

| OBJECTS | LOCATION |
|---|---|
| 1. large white screen | ___on___ the front wall |
| 2. huge whiteboard | __________ the screen |
| 3. clock | __________ the screen |
| 4. light switches | __________ the clock |
| 5. armchairs | __________ the wall |
| 6. instructor's desk | __________ the lecture hall |
| 7. lectern | __________ the desk |
| 8. 30 rows of seats | __________ the teacher's desk |
| 9. small folding tabletop | __________ each seat |
| 10. 3 feet of space | __________ the rows |

**B** **Think about the location of five things in your classroom. On a separate sheet of paper, write a clue to describe where each thing is. Use five different prepositions from Part A. Begin each sentence with *It's* or *They're*.**

1. It's under Mr. Brown's desk.

2. They're on the wall.

**Then read your clues to a partner and ask him or her to guess what you are describing.**

# ORGANIZATION

In this section, you will focus on how to organize descriptive paragraphs. You will learn how to write effective topic and concluding sentences and how to write supporting sentences that include specific details.

## TOPIC SENTENCES AND CONCLUDING SENTENCES

Like the topic sentences of listing-order and how-to paragraphs, the topic sentence of a descriptive paragraph also has a topic and a controlling idea. The topic usually names the person, place, or thing to be described. The controlling idea usually gives a general impression of the topic (*beautiful, neat, messy, interesting, unusual, crowded, busy, noisy*, and so on). Here are some examples of topic sentences for descriptive paragraphs:

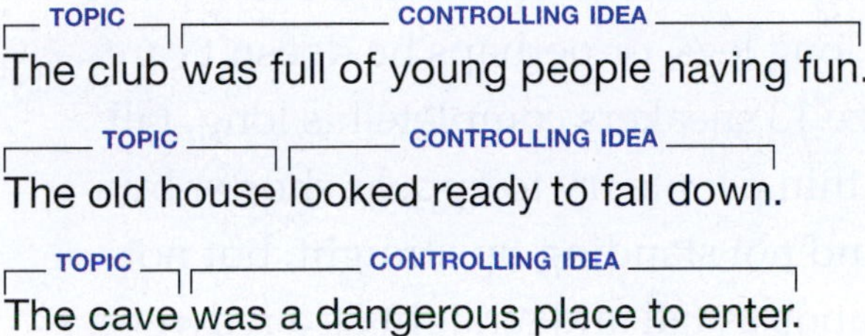


The concluding sentence of a descriptive paragraph can do one of the following:

- It may repeat the idea stated in the topic sentence using different words.

OR

- It may repeat the idea and also give the writer's opinion or feeling about the topic.

Here are examples of concluding sentences that you might use with the topic sentences above:

To sum up, the music, dancing, and flashing lights made the club an exciting and fun place to be. (IDEA IN DIFFERENT WORDS)

In short, I doubt the old house will survive one more winter. (OPINION)

My friend and I were very happy when we got out of the cave. (FEELING)

PRACTICE 3 **Analyzing a Descriptive Paragraph**

**Read the description. Then answer the questions.**

### My Tall Nephew

The first thing you notice about my nephew is that he is extremely tall—6 feet, 6 inches tall, to be exact. His head sticks up almost a foot above everyone else's. His hair is short, light brown, and curly, and his eyes are blue. His nose is long and straight, and his mouth curls into an easy smile. His casual clothes are typical of young people everywhere: a T-shirt and jeans. But what really stands out is how his clothes emphasize how long and thin he is. As your eyes move down, you notice that his jeans sit low on his hips and are just a little too short. Perhaps he can't find pants to fit his narrow waist and long legs, or perhaps he doesn't care much about clothes. His size 13 sneakers complete his long, tall appearance. Some tall and thin people try to appear shorter by rounding their shoulders and not standing up straight, but not my nephew. In short, he stands as tall and straight as a redwood tree, and you can't help thinking, "This is a strong and confident young man."

**1.** What is the topic of the topic sentence? What is the controlling idea?

Topic: ______________________________

Controlling idea: ______________________________

**2.** What word in the topic sentence is repeated in the concluding sentence?

______________________________

**3.** In the concluding sentence, does the writer repeat the idea stated in the topic sentence, or does she express an opinion or feeling about it?

______________________________

**4.** What kind of space order does the writer of this paragraph use? Choose from the list of possibilities on page 110.

______________________________

## SUPPORTING SENTENCES WITH SPECIFIC DETAILS

When you describe something, your goal is to make your reader "see" what you have described. The way to do this is to use supporting sentences that contain specific details. *Specific* means exact or precise. The opposite of specific is general or vague. The more specific you can be, the better your reader can visualize or see what you are describing.

| VAGUE | SPECIFIC |
|---|---|
| a lot of money | $500,000 |
| a large house | a six-bedroom house with four bathrooms |
| a nice car | a red BMW convertible |
| a pretty face | warm brown eyes and sparkling teeth |

**PRACTICE 4** **Adding Specific Details**

**Work with a partner. Add as many specific details as you can to these vague descriptions. Then compare answers with other pairs.**

**1.** My uncle is large.

**a.** He is 6 feet, 3 inches tall and weighs 250 pounds.

**b.** His shirts are XXX Large.

**c.** ______

**d.** ______

**2.** My boss has a beautiful house.

**a.** ______

**b.** ______

**c.** ______

**d.** ______

**3.** Our public library is nice.

**a.** ______

**b.** ______

**c.** ______

**d.** ______

*(continued on next page)*

4. The inside of the taxicab is dirty.

a. ______________________________

b. ______________________________

c. ______________________________

d. ______________________________

5. The student cafeteria is noisy and crowded.

a. ______________________________

b. ______________________________

c. ______________________________

d. ______________________________

**PRACTICE 5** **Revising to Add Specific Details**

**A** **Work with a partner or small group. Study the picture and read "The Student Lounge." Does the writer succeed in making the reader "see" the room? Why or why not? How could the description be improved?**

**The Student Lounge**

During last month's college tour, I was very impressed with the student lounge at the dorm. The lounge was pretty big. In the center, there were some nice couches. To the left, there was a pool table. The lounge had a nice kitchen. There was a TV and a nice study area. The student lounge was really nice.

**B** Rewrite "The Student Lounge" in the space provided, adding more specific details. Decide on the space order you will use, and add at least ten sentences to the beginning. If desired, use some of the nouns and adjectives in the box.

**Nouns**

| | | | |
|---|---|---|---|
| armchair | couch | dining table | refrigerator |
| chairs | counter | lamp | utensils |
| coffee table | cushions | pots and pans | windows |

**Adjectives**

| | | | |
|---|---|---|---|
| black | enjoyable | leather | sunny |
| brand-new | enormous | metal | traditional |
| clean | flat-screen | neat | wooden |
| comfortable | large | small | |

The Student Lounge

During last month's college tour, I was very impressed with the student lounge in the dorm. The lounge was pretty big. It was about 40 feet by 40 feet.

**C** Compare answers with other groups. What specific details did other groups include that were different from yours?

## OUTLINING

In Chapter 3, you practiced using listing and outlining to organize the steps in a "how-to" paragraph. In this section, you will practice using listing and outlining to organize the details of a descriptive paragraph.

After you use listing to get your ideas, the next step is to edit your list and then make an outline. You can do this in three stages:

1. Read your list. Cross out repeated or unimportant ideas.
2. Look at your details. Decide what space order you will use: right to left, front to back, etc. Then number your details in that order.
3. Use your edited list to make an outline.

### PRACTICE 6 Editing a List before Outlining

**Follow these instructions to edit and organize the list that the writer used to create the writing model on page 111.**

1. Edit the list. Put a line through the details that the writer did not include.
2. Decide what space order to use: Number the details to show the order the writer used in the paragraph.

The New Lecture Hall

General impression: beautiful, spacious, modern, comfortable

in the main part, 30 rows of seats

on desk—overhead projector, computer

~~good lighting~~

no windows

1 white screen on wall

2 whiteboard

green carpet

2 armchairs against wall

in back, 2 entrances for students

seats—cushioned and comfortable

each seat: small, folding tabletop

in the front, instructor's desk

electrical outlets near each seat

3 feet of space between rows

lectern

clock and light switches

**PRACTICE 7** **Creating an Outline**

Complete the outline that the writer created from the edited list in Practice 6.

SPACE ORDER: Front to back

TITLE: The New Lecture Hall

TOPIC SENTENCE: Our community college's beautiful new lecture hall is spacious, modern, and comfortable.

MAIN POINTS:

A. On the front wall
- white screen
- ______________________
- ______________________

B. At the front of the lecture hall
- ______________________
- ______________________
- ______________________

C. ______________________________________________
- ______________________
- ______________________
- ______________________

CONCLUDING SENTENCE: To sum up, our new lecture hall is a pleasing and comfortable place to learn.

**TRY IT OUT!** **On a separate sheet of paper, create an outline using one of the two lists you created in Practice 1 on pages 108–109. Follow these directions:**

1. Look at your list and cross out any ideas that you don't want to write about.
2. Decide on the space order you will use, and number your list accordingly.
3. Use your edited list to create an outline.
   a. Write a topic sentence that names the place and tells what kind of person lives or works there. For example, your topic sentence for the office in Picture 2 (on page 109) might be one of these:

      The office of one of the best instructors at my school is neat and well-organized.

      It's not surprising that one of our school's most successful and well-respected professors works in this tidy office.

   b. Using capital letters (A, B, C, and so on), write down the details from your edited list.
   c. Write a concluding sentence that tells your feeling or opinion about the place. For example, you could write:

      This instructor's office is a perfect place to work or to talk with students.

4. Use your outline to write a descriptive paragraph.
5. Proofread your paragraph and correct any mistakes. You will use this paragraph again in Practice 14.

## GRAMMAR

In this chapter, you will learn how to use adjectives to make a description more vivid and interesting.

### ADJECTIVES

Adjectives describe nouns and pronouns. Adjectives tell what things (or people) look like, what kind they are, or how many or how much there are. Adjectives answer the questions: *What kind? Which one?* and *How many/much?*

| | | |
|---|---|---|
| What kind? | The **old** car has a **broken** window. | |
| | He's **smart** and **funny**. | |
| Which one? | the **red** dress | the **fourth** chapter of the book |
| How many/much? | **five** students | not **much** homework |

Read the chart to learn some things about adjectives.

| ADJECTIVES | EXAMPLES |
|---|---|
| **1.** Adjectives come in front of nouns, not after them. | The talented young musicians |
| **2.** Adjectives can also follow linking verbs. | be — The children are happy.<br>seem — You seem sad.<br>look — Brides always look beautiful.<br>smell — The cookies smell delicious.<br>taste — Candy tastes sweet.<br>feel — Silk feels smooth. |
| **3.** Adjectives have only one form. Use the same adjective with singular and plural nouns. | a terrible storm<br>terrible storms (*not* terribles storms)<br>a cute child<br>cute children (*not* cutes children) |
| **4.** A compound adjective is two or more words that function as an adjective. A compound adjective often has a hyphen or hyphens between its parts. | a one-hour drive<br>a part-time job<br>a reddish-gold sunset |
| **5.** In compound adjectives with hyphenated number-noun combinations, the noun is always singular. | a five-dollar bill (*not* a five-dollars bill)<br>a two-year-old child (*not* a two-years-old child)<br>a six-foot-high wall (*not* a six-feet-high wall) |
| **6.** Some nouns can also function as adjectives. | the English book — tennis balls<br>a shoe store — the Japanese students |
| **7.** Proper adjectives (that is, adjectives referring to nationalities, languages, places, and so on) are capitalized. | an Egyptian custom — my Spanish class<br>the Cuban government — Asian languages |
| **8.** Present and past participles can be used as adjectives. | a boring class — bored students<br>a cooking class — a cooked meal<br>breaking news — a broken heart<br>a swimming pool — the stolen money |

**PRACTICE 8** **Identifying Adjectives**

Read the paragraph. Circle the adjectives. (HINT: Do not circle possessive adjectives such as *my* and *its*.)

### My First Car

My first car was old and ugly, but I loved it anyway. It was a very bright shade of blue, but it also had green, yellow, and gray paint in different places. The body was in terrible condition. It had several big dents[1]. The lock on the hood was broken, so I had to tie down the hood with a strong rope. Also, the back bumper was rusty, and the front window had a big crack in it. The inside of the car was also in bad condition. The door handle on the passenger side was broken, so you couldn't open the passenger door from the inside. The seats had at least ten large holes in them. Also, the gas gauge was stuck. It always showed "full," so I often ran out of gas. The speedometer was broken too, so I never knew how quickly I was driving. My old VW had many faults[2], but in my mind it was perfect.

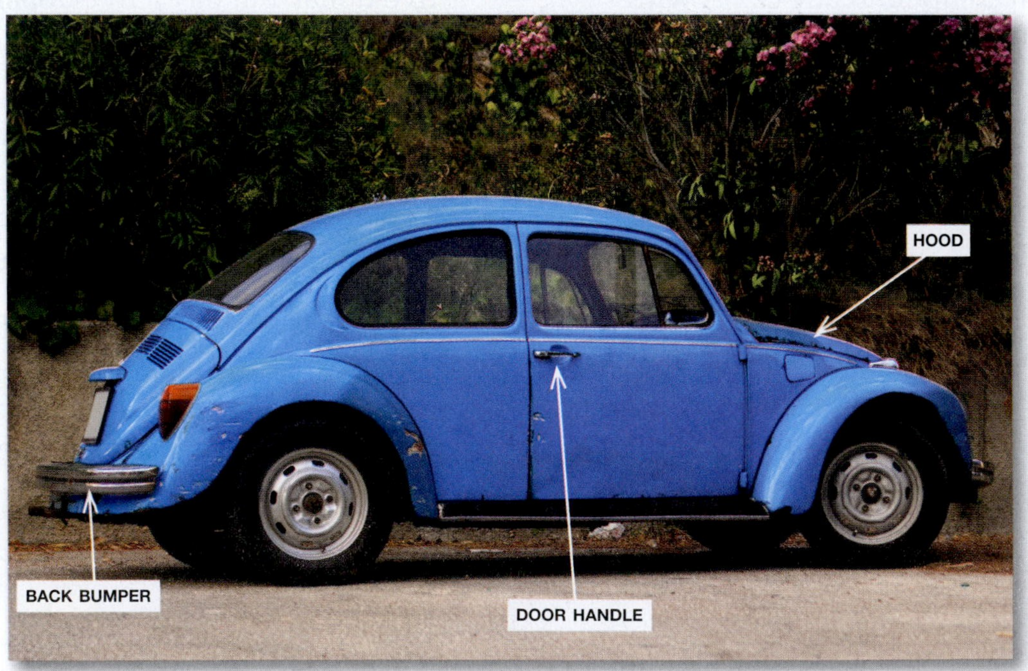


[1] **dents:** marks made when you hit or press something into a surface

[2] **faults:** flaws; problems; bad or nonworking parts

## ORDER OF ADJECTIVES

When you use adjectives to describe a noun, you may put several adjectives before the noun. Sometimes you must put them in a particular order, and sometimes you can choose your own order depending on the kind of adjective. Cumulative adjectives must be in a particular order while the order of coordinate adjectives can vary.

| CUMULATIVE ADJECTIVES | COORDINATE ADJECTIVES |
|---|---|
| The **poor little black** dog | The **wet, cold,** and **hungry** dog |
| | The **hungry, wet,** and **cold** dog |
| | The **cold, wet,** and **hungry** dog |

### Cumulative Adjectives

Cumulative adjectives always go before a noun. They must be in a particular order. For example, you cannot write *the little black poor dog*; you **must** write *the poor little black dog*. Do not put commas between cumulative adjectives.

Here is a chart showing the order of cumulative adjectives:

| KIND OF ADJECTIVE | EXAMPLES |
|---|---|
| **1.** Quantity | two, fifty, some, many, (a) few |
| **2.** Opinion | poor, beautiful, interesting, cheerful, expensive |
| **3.** Appearance<br>• Size<br>• Age<br>• Shape/Length<br>• Condition<br>• Color | <br>big, little<br>old, new, young<br>round, square, short, long<br>rusty, broken, hungry, wet, cold<br>black, red, blond |
| **4.** Origin or nationality | Guatemalan, European, Congolese, Asian |
| **5.** Material | silk, wood, cotton, gold, metal |
| **6.** Kind/use/purpose | shoe (as in *shoe store*), wedding (as in *wedding dress*) swimming, reading, hiking |

**Writing Tip**

In general, do not use more than two or three adjectives before a noun. Using too many adjectives in a row weakens your description and may confuse the reader. In the following example, the second sentence is more effective.

The poor little **hungry** black dog was lost. *(four adjectives before noun)*

The poor little black dog was lost and **hungry**. *(three adjectives before noun)*

## PRACTICE 9 Working with Cumulative Adjectives

**Rewrite each sentence using the adjectives in parentheses to describe the underlined noun. Refer to the chart on page 123 to help you determine the order.**

1. There were toys in the middle of the floor. (broken, several, plastic)

   *There were several broken plastic toys in the middle of the floor.*

2. We left the beach when we saw the clouds. (black, big)

   ______________________________

3. Flags hung from every window. (colorful, rectangular)

   ______________________________

4. Children played on the grass. (green, thick)

   ______________________________

5. I dream about relaxing on a beach. (Mexican, white, beautiful)

   ______________________________

6. They plan to fix up the car. (Italian, expensive, small)

   ______________________________

7. The parents left their children with the grandparents. (young, two)

   ______________________________

8. The real estate agent pointed out problems with the house. (minor, several)

   ______________________________

## Coordinate Adjectives

Coordinate adjectives can go before a noun or after a linking verb. You can write coordinate adjectives in any order, and you can separate them from each other with commas. Also:

- When coordinate adjectives come before a noun, you may put the word *and* before the last one (but you don't have to).

  BEFORE A NOUN: A **hungry, cold, wet** dog sat outside our front door.

  (OPTIONAL): A **wet, cold,** and **hungry** dog sat outside our front door.

- When two or more coordinate adjectives come after a linking verb, you must put *and* before the last one.

  AFTER A LINKING VERB (REQUIRED): The dog was **hungry, wet,** and **cold**.

**PRACTICE 10** **Using Commas with Coordinate Adjectives**

**Read the sentences. Add commas as needed.**

1. The people want a smart, experienced, honest leader.
2. Most students like friendly enthusiastic imaginative teachers.
3. I am tired of the cold rainy weather.
4. I am looking forward to the warm sunny relaxing days of summer.
5. The prince in a fairy tale is either tall dark and handsome or tall blond and handsome.

**PRACTICE 11** **Identifying Cumulative and Coordinate Adjectives**

**Underline and identify each adjective. Write *1* for cumulative and *2* for coordinate. Add commas where needed.**

1. I found a small green piece of smelly, moldy[1] cheese under my bed.
2. Four shiny black limousines were parked outside the hotel.
3. The small red apples looked sweet crisp juicy and delicious.
4. Hundreds of happy cheering football fans ran onto the field.
5. The new young French teacher is from Quebec.
6. My father bought my mother a beautiful antique Persian rug as a gift for their 20th wedding anniversary.

**PRACTICE 12** **Correcting Adjective Errors**

**Work alone or with a partner. Find the errors in adjective order or comma usage in each sentence. Make corrections.**

1. The hungry, black cat waited for someone to feed him.
2. The big, brown dog waited for his owner to come out of the store grocery.
3. We bought a chocolate delicious cake for my brother's little birthday.
4. For his tenth birthday, he received a metal new baseball bat.
5. Our coach's enthusiastic supportive manner gave our team confidence.

[1] **moldy:** covered with a soft green or black substance (as on old bread)

**PRACTICE 13** **Writing Sentences with Adjectives**

**Write sentences describing objects you might find under the bed of a very messy teenager. Use at least two adjectives to describe each object.**

1. Under the bed, I saw several fuzzy dust balls.
2. I also saw a pair of ______________________.
3. Then I discovered a box of ______________________.
4. Next to it, I found a greasy paper bag with ______________ inside it.
5. The discovery of ______________________ didn't surprise me.

**PRACTICE 14** **Revising Your Writing with Adjectives**

**Use the paragraph you wrote in the Try It Out! activity on page 120. Follow the directions to revise your paragraph.**

1. Reread your paragraph. Where possible, add adjectives to your sentences to make your writing more descriptive. For example:

   There is a ^shiny silver^ laptop on the ^old-fashioned wooden^ desk.

2. Rewrite your paragraph. Proofread it carefully. Check for the correct order of adjectives and use of commas.

## SENTENCE STRUCTURE

In this chapter, you will look at how to use prepositional phrases in different positions in a sentence.

### PREPOSITIONS

**Prepositions** are words such as *of*, *to*, *from*, *in*, and *at*. Most prepositions are one word. A few prepositions are two words (*next to*) or three words (*in front of*). Here is a list of common prepositions:

| | | | | | |
|---|---|---|---|---|---|
| above | behind | during | of | throughout | according to |
| across | below | except | off | till | because of |
| after | beneath | for | on | to | next to |
| against | beside | from | out | toward | out of |
| along | between | in | outside | until | in addition to |
| around | beyond | inside | over | upon | in back of |
| at | by | into | since | with | in front of |
| before | down | near | through | without | in place of |

## PREPOSITIONAL PHRASES

A preposition is usually combined with a noun or noun phrase to make a **prepositional phrase**, such as *in the house* or *at six o'clock*. Here are some common types of prepositional phrases:

- **Prepositional phrases of place** answer the question *Where?* These are useful in space-order paragraphs to show the location of objects in a description.

| | |
|---|---|
| on the desk | opposite the door |
| next to the window | in the closet |
| under the bed | in the middle of the room |
| in front of the house | in the distance |

- **Prepositional phrases of time** answer the question *When?* These are useful in "how-to" paragraphs to give the order of the steps.

| | |
|---|---|
| at the beginning | before the test |
| after that | upon arrival |
| after class | in the morning |
| on New Year's Day | at midnight |

- **Prepositional phrases of possession** answer the question *Whose?*

| | |
|---|---|
| (the father) of the bride | (the colors) of the rainbow |
| (the name) of my boss | (the director) of the company |

- Other prepositional phrases describe or identify someone or something. They answer the question *Which one/ones?*

| | |
|---|---|
| (the boy) with red hair | (the men) in the blue uniforms |
| (a glass) of water | (the students) from Ecuador |

**PRACTICE 15** **Identifying Prepositional Phrases**

**A** **Read the paragraph. Underline each preposition. Then put parentheses around the prepositional phrases.**

### My Desk

1 Some (of my friends) think the inside (of my desk drawers) resembles a second-hand store. 2 In the long center drawer under my computer, you can find paper clips, erasers, pencils, pens, rubber bands, and small bottles of glue. 3 To the right of this large drawer, there are four smaller drawers. 4 In the one at the top, I have a bunch of tools. 5 If you want to repair something, you can find whatever you need there. 6 In the second drawer, I keep snacks so I don't get hungry at night. 7 Small items of clothing are in the third drawer, and the bottom drawer holds my collection of wind-up toys. 8 The toys help me relax during my study breaks. 9 According to my friends, I have such a variety of things in my desk that I could start a small business.

**B** **Work with a partner. Answer the questions.**

1. The paragraph in Part A has 17 prepositional phrases (not including the examples in the first sentence). Compare answers. Did you find them all?
2. Which four sentences begin with prepositional phrases that tell where something is? ______________________________
3. Which two sentences have a prepositional phrase of place that is not at the start of the sentence? ______________________________
4. The writer uses two different kinds of space order. What are they?

   Sentences 1–3: ______________________________

   Sentences 4–9: ______________________________

## Using Prepositional Phrases to Vary Sentence Beginnings

A paragraph in which every sentence follows the same subject–verb–object pattern can be boring. One way to vary and improve your writing is to start some of your sentences with prepositional phrases of time and place. When you do this, you should put a comma after the opening prepositional phrase.

USUAL PATTERN: Get eight hours of sleep **before a big exam**.

VARIATION: **Before a big exam,** get eight hours of sleep.

USUAL PATTERN: I keep snacks **in the second drawer**.

VARIATION: **In the second drawer,** I keep snacks.

You can also vary the pattern in sentences that contain *there is/there are* and *there was/there were*. Again, add a comma when you move a prepositional phrase to the beginning of the sentence.

USUAL PATTERN: There is a secret hiding place **under the stairs**.

VARIATION: **Under the stairs,** there is a secret hiding place.

USUAL PATTERN: There are several kinds of trees **in the park**.

VARIATION: **In the park,** there are several kinds of trees.

Sometimes the subject of a sentence can just change places with a prepositional phrase of place. This is possible only when the sentence contains a subject, an intransitive verb (a verb that has no object), and a prepositional phrase of place. In this case, do not add a comma when you start with the prepositional phrase.

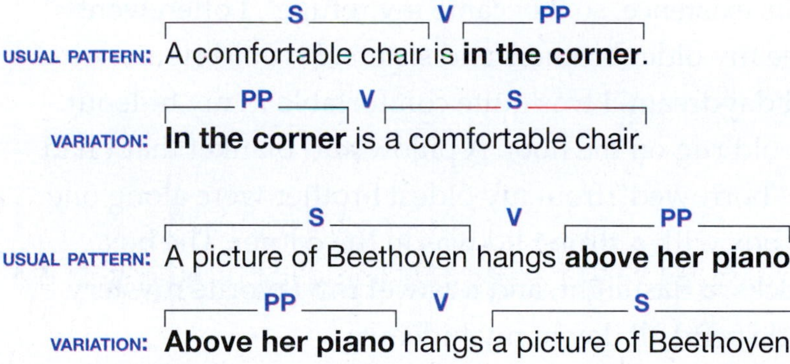

USUAL PATTERN: A comfortable chair is **in the corner**.

VARIATION: **In the corner** is a comfortable chair.

USUAL PATTERN: A picture of Beethoven hangs **above her piano**.

VARIATION: **Above her piano** hangs a picture of Beethoven.

**PRACTICE 16** Identifying and Punctuating Prepositional Phrases

**A** Read the paragraph. Then put parentheses around all prepositional phrases. Add a comma after prepositional phrases of time and place that begin a sentence.

### My Favorite Place

My favorite place on the campus of our school is the lawn in front of the library. During my lunch break I go there to relax with friends. In the center of the lawn there is a fountain. Water splashes from the fountain onto some rocks around it. The sound of the splashing water reminds me of a place in the mountains where we go in the summer. Under a group of trees at the edge of the lawn are wooden benches and tables. On warm days students sit at the tables in the shade of the trees to eat their lunches. The chatter[1] of students makes studying impossible. After lunch it becomes quiet again.

**B** Read the paragraph. Put parentheses around prepositional phrases of time and place. Then rewrite the paragraph in the space provided on page 131. Vary the structure of two or three of the sentences with one of the variations on page 129.

### My Childhood Hideout[2]

I had a secret hiding place near my childhood home. No one knew of its existence, so it became my refuge[3]. I often went there to escape my older brothers and sisters. I would sit alone for hours and daydream. I was quite comfortable in my hideout. There was an old rug on the floor. A pillow and blanket that I had permanently "borrowed" from my oldest brother were along one wall. A metal box with a strong lid was in the corner. The box contained snacks, a flashlight, and a few of my favorite mystery novels. I could spend all day in my hideout.

[1] **chatter:** noisy talking
[2] **hideout:** hiding place
[3] **refuge:** place of safety

My Childhood Hideout

## PRACTICE 17 Combining Sentences

**Combine the sentences in each group into one sentence. For some, there may be more than one answer.**

**1. a.** The old lecture hall is dark.

**b.** The old lecture hall is old-fashioned.

The old lecture hall is dark and old-fashioned.

**2. a.** There's a chalkboard.

**b.** The chalkboard is green.

**c.** The chalkboard is cracked.

**d.** The chalkboard is on the wall.

**3. a.** There are several maps on the wall.

**b.** The maps are outdated.

**c.** There's a clock on the wall.

**d.** The clock is big.

*(continued on next page)*

4. **a.** In front of the chalkboard there is a desk.
   **b.** The desk is metal.
   **c.** The desk is large.
   **d.** The desk is scratched.

   ______________________________________________

   ______________________________________________

5. **a.** For the students, there are rows of chairs.
   **b.** There are 20 rows.
   **c.** The chairs are blue.
   **d.** The chairs are plastic.
   **e.** The chairs are uncomfortable.

   ______________________________________________

   ______________________________________________

## Applying Vocabulary: Using Prepositions of Place

Before you begin your writing assignment, review what you learned about prepositions of place on page 112.

### PRACTICE 18 Using Prepositions of Place

**Use words and phrases from the box to complete each sentence. Add nouns as needed (for example, a room or piece of furniture). For 7 and 8, write about other items in your living room or the student lounge.**

| | | |
|---|---|---|
| **against** | **between** | **on** |
| **at the front (of)** | **in front of** | **on the left/right (of)** |
| **behind** | **in the center (of)** | **to the left/right of (of)** |
| **beneath** | **next to** | **underneath** |

1. In my bedroom, my *desk is on the left, next to the window*.
2. ______________ my ______________, ______________.
3. The kitchen is located ______________.
4. ______________, the refrigerator, ______________.
5. The living room/student lounge is ______________.

6. ______________________ the living room/student lounge, there
______________________________________________.

7. ______________________________________________.

8. ______________________________________________.

## WRITING ASSIGNMENT

In this chapter, your assignment is to write a descriptive paragraph about a place that is special to you. As an alternative, you can choose one of the topic suggestions from the list. Use space order to organize your ideas. Follow the steps in the writing process.

**Topic Suggestions**

- Your classroom
- The student cafeteria
- Your favorite room in your house
- Your grandmother's kitchen
- Your neighborhood
- A crowded bus on a hot day
- The subway at rush hour
- The town square on market day
- A club on a weekend night
- A beach at sunset
- Your dream house
- A holiday parade

### STEP 1: Prewrite to get ideas.

- Use listing to get ideas. Think about the place you have chosen and the general impression you want to create. Then list as many details as you can about the place.
- When you are done, edit your list by crossing out any ideas that you don't want to write about. Next, think about what space order you will use and number your list accordingly.
- Make an outline. Your outline should include all three parts of a paragraph: a topic sentence, supporting ideas, and a concluding sentence. For each supporting idea, list specific details such as descriptive words and words that describe location.
- Review the prepositions of place in Looking at Vocabulary and Applying Vocabulary on pages 112 and 132–133. Look at your outline again and, if possible, add in some of these (or similar) words.

**Writing Tip**

At the prewriting stage, some writers find it useful to make a quick drawing of the place they want to describe. Making a drawing can help you remember details such as where things are and what something looks like.

## STEP 2: Write the first draft.

- Write *FIRST DRAFT* at the top of your paper.
- Follow your outline to write your paragraph.
- Add adjectives and prepositional phrases of place where possible to make your description more specific.
- Try to include at least three sentences that begin with prepositional phrases of place.

## STEP 3: Revise and edit the first draft.

- Exchange papers with a partner and give each other feedback on your paragraphs. Use Chapter 4 Peer Review on page 212.
- Consider your partner's feedback and revise your paragraph. Mark changes on your first draft.
- Check your paragraph carefully against Chapter 4 Writer's Self-Check on page 213, and continue to make changes as necessary.

## STEP 4: Write a new draft.

- Refer to the changes you made on your first draft and do a final draft of your paragraph.
- Proofread it carefully.
- Hand it in to your teacher. Your teacher may also ask you to hand in your prewriting, your outline, and your first draft.

## SELF-ASSESSMENT

**In this chapter, you learned to:**

- ❍ Use listing to get ideas for describing a place
- ❍ Organize a descriptive paragraph using space order
- ❍ Develop a description with specific details
- ❍ Identify adjectives and use them in the correct order
- ❍ Vary the structure of sentences with prepositional phrases
- ❍ Write, revise, and edit a descriptive paragraph

**Which ones can you do well? Mark them** ✓

**Which ones do you need to practice more? Mark them** ✗

# EXPANSION

## TIMED WRITING

To succeed in academic writing you need to be able to write quickly and fluently. For example, you might have to write a paragraph for a test in class, and you only have 30 minutes. In this activity, you will write a paragraph in class. You will have 30 minutes. To complete the activity in time, follow the directions.

1. Read the prompt below (or the prompt your teacher assigns) carefully. Make sure you understand the question or task. Then decide on the topic of your paragraph. (3 minutes)
2. Use listing to get ideas for the details you will write about. Then read over your list and decide which ideas you will write about. Edit your list and then make an outline to organize your ideas. (8 minutes)
3. Write your paragraph. Be sure to include a title, a topic sentence, supporting ideas, adjectives, prepositional phrases of place in a variety of positions, and a concluding sentence. (15 minutes)
4. Proofread your paragraph. Correct any mistakes. (4 minutes)
5. Give your paper to your teacher.

**Prompt:** Describe a popular outdoor public space, such as a park, a plaza, or a square. Describe where things are and what people enjoy doing there. Use space-order organization.

## YOUR JOURNAL

Continue making entries in your journal. If you cannot think of a topic for a journal entry, try one of these ideas:

- Describe a special place where you stayed during vacation or while on a trip. Describe the place in as much detail as possible.
- Describe a room in a relative's house. Describe the place in detail and explain why it is a special place for you.

*For more ideas for journal entries, see Appendix A on page 193.*

# CHAPTER 5

# STATING REASONS AND USING EXAMPLES

## OBJECTIVES

**Writers need certain skills.**

**In this chapter, you will learn to:**

- Use listing and outlining to brainstorm and organize ideas
- Develop a paragraph with reasons and examples
- Write effective conclusion sentences
- Use complex sentences with reason and condition clauses
- Apply more rules of capitalization and comma usage
- Write, revise, and edit a paragraph with reasons and examples

*Costa Rica is a great place to spend a semester doing research for a number of reasons. Can you think of some?*

## INTRODUCTION

In this chapter, you will learn how to write a listing-order paragraph using reasons and examples to support your ideas. You will also learn about complex sentences with reason clauses and condition clauses. Finally, you will learn additional rules related to capitalization and commas.

To help you get ideas for writing, you will first do some prewriting.

## PREWRITING

In Chapters 3 and 4, you used listing and outlining to brainstorm and organize ideas for steps in a "how-to" paragraph and for details in a descriptive paragraph. In this chapter, you will use listing and outlining to brainstorm and organize ideas for a paragraph with reasons and examples.

### LISTING AND OUTLINING WITH REASONS AND EXAMPLES

In this section, you will practice using listing and outlining to organize the ideas. You will follow three steps: (1) listing reasons and examples, (2) editing your list and adding more information, if necessary, and (3) organizing your list into an outline.

**PRACTICE 1** **From List to Outline**

**A** A friend asked you to recommend a place to study English. With a partner or a small group, discuss various schools and reasons your friend should consider them. Consider things such as:

location
cost
courses
instructors
student body
success rate
equipment (computers, etc.)
cultural excursions

**B** Choose one of the schools you discussed in Part A. Follow the directions.

1. List reasons.
   - Use listing to brainstorm as many reasons as you can to support your recommendation.

Reasons to Study at ____________________

| Reasons | Examples |
| --- | --- |
| | |
| | |
| | |
| | |
| | |
| | |
| | |

2. List examples.
   - In the right-hand column, add one or two specific examples for each reason you listed: for example, the name of a specific course, the cost of classes, a special program, or details about what makes the location convenient.
3. Edit the list.
   - Cross out any ideas that you don't want to write about.
   - Add more supporting details, as needed.
   - Number your reasons to show the order they will appear in your outline.

4. Organize your list into an outline.
   - Use your list to complete the outline. You can write phrases or complete sentences.
   - Add a topic sentence. (You will be given a chance to add a concluding sentence later on.)

   Save your outline to use in the Try It Out! activity on page 150.

| | |
|---|---|
| TITLE | Reasons to Study at ________ |
| TOPIC SENTENCE | ________ is a good place to study English for several reasons. |
| 1ST REASON | A. |
| EXAMPLES | 1. |
| | 2. |
| 2ND REASON | B. |
| EXAMPLES | 1. |
| | 2. |
| 3RD REASON | C. |
| EXAMPLES | 1. |
| | 2. |
| 4TH REASON | D. |
| EXAMPLES | 1. |
| | 2. |

## PARAGRAPHS WITH REASONS AND EXAMPLES

When writing a paragraph of recommendation, you use reasons and examples to support your main idea. Here are the keys to writing a well-organized paragraph:

- State your recommendation in your topic sentence.
- Give several reasons for your recommendation. Your reasons tell why you are making the recommendation.
- Support each reason with examples.
- End with a concluding sentence restating your recommendation.

## LOOKING AT THE MODEL

The writing model discusses reasons to study wildlife in Costa Rica.

**Work with a partner or in a small group. Read the model. Then answer the questions.**

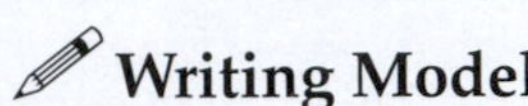

**Writing Model**

### Costa Rica: A Great Place to Study Wildlife

Costa Rica is a great place to spend a semester doing wildlife research for two reasons. First of all, this small country has very diverse[1] geography, so it has many different wildlife habitats. For example, Tortuguero National Park, on Costa Rica's northeastern coast, has more than ten different wildlife habitats, including rainforests, beaches, swamps, and canals. Students can study alligators in the swamps or observe sea turtles as they lay their eggs on the beaches. Another example is Corcovado National Park on the west coast. With its 13 different habitats, including an ancient rainforest, it is one of the most important nature preserves of the American continents. Second, Costa Rica has an astounding number of wildlife species[2]. For instance, near the Arenal Volcano, there are 135 species of reptiles, including tortoises, snakes, and lizards, and over 250 species of birds live in the area. Another place with a rich variety of wildlife is Corcovado. There students can observe exotic animals, such as anteaters, spider monkeys, jaguars, and over 360 species of birds. Indeed, Costa Rica is a wonderful place to study if you love wildlife.

[1] **diverse:** showing great variety

[2] **species:** types of animals or plants (the same form is used for both singular and plural)

### Questions about the Model

1. What is the controlling idea?
2. What are the writer's exact reasons?
3. What transition signal does he use to introduce each reason?
4. How many examples does the writer use to support each reason? What words signal each example?
5. Does the concluding sentence restate the recommendation or the reasons?
6. What organizational pattern does the writer use: space order, time order, or listing order?

## Looking at Vocabulary: Words that Describe Geography

When you describe a place, you will often use words to describe its geography. Geographical terms have very specific definitions, so it is important to know exactly what each term means. For example, both a stream and a canal are like small rivers of water, but a stream is shallow, rocky, and natural while a canal is deep and made by humans.

### PRACTICE 2 Looking at Words that Describe Geography

**A** Look at the writing model. Find and underline the words from the box. (The words are in the order that they appear in the model.)

| | | | |
|---|---|---|---|
| habitats | ~~rainforests~~ | swamps | continents |
| coast | beaches | canals | volcano |

**B** Complete the sentences with words from the box in Part A. If needed, use a dictionary to help you.

1. According to an article I read, rainforests cover only 6% of the Earth's surface, yet they contain more than 50% of the planet's plant and animal species.
2. People associate the name Ferdinand de Lesseps with the building of both the Suez and Panama _______________.
3. The states of California, Oregon, and Washington are on the west _______________ of the United States.
4. Visitors to Hawaii can often see streams of hot lava flowing into the ocean at night from Kilauea, the island's most active _______________.

*(continued on next page)*

5. The ________________ in California are famous for surfing, high waves, and rocky cliffs and shores.

6. ________________ are low-lying areas of wetland that are home to mosquitoes, alligators, snakes, and a wide variety of other wildlife.

7. Deserts are one of the most extreme ________________ on earth, so it's surprising to learn they are home to a wide variety of plant and animal life.

8. Most people think of Asia and Europe as two different ________________, but in fact they are one large area of land that some people call Eurasia.

## ORGANIZATION

In this section, you will look at how to organize a paragraph with reasons and examples. You will also learn how to write effective topic and concluding sentences and how to use transition signals for reasons, conditions, and examples.

### REASONS AND EXAMPLES

When you write a topic sentence such as *Costa Rica is a great place to spend a semester doing wildlife research*, you need to support it with **reasons** to help convince your readers. You then need to support your reasons with **specific examples**.

The author of the writing model gives two main reasons to explain why Costa Rica is a great place to spend a semester studying wildlife:

- It has very diverse geography, so it has many different wildlife habitats.
- It has an astounding number of wildlife species.

The writer supports each reason with two examples. The examples are specific facts about specific places. To support his first reason, he talks about the number and kinds of habitats in Tortuguero and Corcovado. To support his second reason, he mentions specific facts about the range and number of various wildlife species near Arenal Volcano and Corcovado.

**PRACTICE 3** **Identifying Examples and Details**

Look at the outline of the writing model. The outline has two main points, reasons A and B. Each reason is supported with two examples that are supported by details. Reread the model on page 140 and complete the missing information in the outline.

TITLE — Costa Rica: A Great Place to Study Wildlife

TOPIC SENTENCE — Costa Rica is a great place to spend a semester doing wildlife research for two reasons.

1ST REASON — A. Very diverse geography

EXAMPLE 1 — 1. Tortuguero National Park (on ____________ coast)

DETAILS —
- a. more than ____________ habitats
- b. swamps - study alligators
- c. beaches - ____________

EXAMPLE 2 — 2. ____________ National Park

DETAILS —
- a. ____________ different habitats
- b. ____________ rainforest
- c. one of the most important preserves on the ____________

2ND REASON — B. Astounding number of wildlife species

EXAMPLE 1 — 1. area near the Arenal Volcano

DETAILS —
- a. ____________ species of reptiles (tortoises, snakes, lizards)
- b. ____________

EXAMPLE 2 — 2. ____________

DETAILS —
- a. Exotic ____________
- b. ____________ species of birds

CONCLUDING SENTENCE — Indeed, Costa Rica is a wonderful place to study if you love wildlife.

**PRACTICE 4** **Identifying and Organizing Reasons and Examples**

Use sentences a–h to complete the outline. (HINT: Identify the two reasons first and then the examples. The examples under each reason can be in any order.)

**a.** A beach community offers recreation for residents of all ages.

**b.** To enjoy the beach, people don't need to have anything special—just a swimsuit, a towel, and sunscreen.

**c.** If you live near a beach, you can easily take a picnic lunch or dinner there.

**d.** For adults, the beach is a great place to just relax or go for a walk.

**e.** It costs very little money to enjoy time at the beach.

**f.** Teenagers can do sports, such as surfing and volleyball.

**g.** Often the parking is free or residents can get parking stickers.

**h.** Children love to splash in the water, jump in the waves, and play in the sand.

TITLE — Living in a Beach Community

TOPIC SENTENCE — There are two reasons why beach communities are great places to live.

1ST REASON — A.

EXAMPLES — 1.

2.

3.

2ND REASON — B.

EXAMPLES — 1.

2.

3.

CONCLUDING SENTENCE — To sum up, beach communities offer great recreation at low prices.

## PRACTICE 5 Giving Specific Examples

Work with a partner. Use your imagination to add reasons and examples to the outline. Write two specific examples for each reason. Use complete sentences.

| | |
|---|---|
| TITLE | The Best Restaurant in Town |
| TOPIC SENTENCE | Joe's Diner is the best restaurant in town. |
| 1ST REASON | A. The food is delicious. |
| EXAMPLES | 1. Joe's double cheeseburger is juicy and full of flavor. |
| | 2. |
| 2ND REASON | B. The service is fast and cheerful. |
| EXAMPLES | 1. |
| | 2. |
| 3RD REASON | C. The prices are low. |
| EXAMPLES | 1. |
| | 2. |
| CONCLUDING SENTENCE | Indeed, if you're looking for great food, amazing service, and reasonable prices, Joe's Diner is the place to go. |

**B** Work alone. Think of a local restaurant to write about. Add reasons and examples to support your topic sentence. Don't worry about adding a concluding sentence at this time. You will add one in Practice 8 on page 150.

| | |
|---|---|
| TITLE | The Worst Restaurant in Town |
| TOPIC SENTENCE | ______________________ is the worst fast-food restaurant in town.<br>(add name) |
| 1ST REASON | A. |
| EXAMPLES | 1. |
| | 2. |
| 2ND REASON | B. |
| EXAMPLES | 1. |
| | 2. |
| 3RD REASON | C. |
| EXAMPLES | 1. |
| | 2. |

## TRANSITION SIGNALS THAT INTRODUCE REASONS

When you use reasons to support a topic sentence, you should introduce each one with a **transition signal**. There are two patterns that you can use to do this:

> PATTERN 1: **First of all, ______.**
>
> **Second, ______.**

This pattern uses a listing-order transition signal at the start of each reason: *first, first of all, second, third, finally,* and so forth.

**First of all,** this small country has very diverse geography, so it has many different wildlife habitats.

**Second,** Costa Rica has an astounding number of wildlife species.

**PATTERN 2:** The **first** reason is ______.

The **second** reason is ______.

This pattern uses the transition word in the subject.

There are two ways to complete a sentence that uses this pattern:

- With a noun phrase[1]:

  The first reason is **diverse geography and many wildlife habitats.**

  The second reason is **Costa Rica's astounding number of wildlife species.**

- With a noun clause[2] (*that* + subject + verb)

  The first reason is **that Costa Rica has a diverse geography and many wildlife habitats**.

  The second reason is **that Costa Rica has an astounding number of wildlife species**.

**PRACTICE 6** **Using Transition Signals to Introduce Reasons**

**Here are three reasons to visit San José, the capital of Costa Rica. Rewrite each reason twice: first, with a listing-order transition signal, and then with a transition signal in the subject.**

**Reason 1:** San José has a pleasant climate.

**a.** First, San José has a pleasant climate.

**b.** The first reason is that San José has a pleasant climate.

**Reason 2:** Hotels and restaurants are inexpensive.

**a.** ______________________________

**b.** ______________________________

**Reason 3:** The people are friendly to tourists.

**a.** ______________________________

**b.** ______________________________

[1] **noun phrase:** group of words ending with a noun that belong together in meaning: for example, *the old house, a good book, several friends*

[2] **noun clause:** a dependent clause that functions in this pattern as complement after a linking verb: for example, *The first reason is* <u>*that Miami has beautiful beaches*</u>.

## TRANSITION SIGNALS THAT INTRODUCE EXAMPLES

There are three transition signals that you can use to introduce examples: *for example*, *for instance*, and *such as*. Notice these patterns:

| PATTERN 1: | **For example,** (+ *sentence*) |
|---|---|
| | **For instance,** (+ *sentence*) |

**Writing Tip**

Be careful when you begin a sentence with *For example* or *For instance*. Make sure your sentence follows either Pattern 1 or Pattern 2.

When your example is a complete sentence, begin the sentence with *For example* or *For instance*. These two transition signals have exactly the same meaning. Put them at the beginning of the sentence and follow them with a comma.[1]

**For example,** Tortuguero National Park has more than ten different wildlife habitats.

**For instance,** Tortuguero National Park has more than ten different wildlife habitats.

| PATTERN 2: | ______, **such as** (+ *nouns*) |
|---|---|
| | ______, **for example** (+ *nouns*) |
| | ______, **for instance** (+ *nouns*) |

When your example is one or more nouns that appear at the end of a sentence, precede it with *such as*, *for example*, or *for instance*. Note these rules:

- Put a comma before *such as*.

  Students can observe exotic animals, **such as** anteaters and spider monkeys.

- Put a comma before and after *for example* and *for instance*.

  Students can observe exotic animals, **for example,** anteaters and spider monkeys.

  Students can observe exotic animals, **for instance,** anteaters and spider monkeys.

| DO NOT DO THIS: | DO THIS: |
|---|---|
| The restaurant specializes in shellfish. For example, fresh lobster and crab. | The restaurant specializes in shellfish. For example, it serves fresh lobster and crab. (PATTERN 1)<br>The restaurant specializes in shellfish, such as fresh lobster and crab. (PATTERN 2)<br>The restaurant specializes in shellfish, for example, fresh lobster and crab. (PATTERN 2) |

[1] *For example* and *for instance* can also appear after the subject or at the end of an example that is a complete sentence. Note the use of commas in each case:

Tortuguero National Park, **for example,** has more than ten different wildlife habitats.

Tortuguero National Park, **for instance,** has more than ten different wildlife habitats.

Tortuguero National Park has more than ten different wildlife habitats, **for example.**

Tortuguero National Park has more than ten different wildlife habitats, **for instance.**

**PRACTICE 7** **Using Transition Signals to Introduce Examples**

**A** **Add commas to the sentences.**

1. Denmark has many children's attractions, such as Tivoli Gardens and Legoland.
2. Japan is famous for its beautiful gardens. For example the rock garden of Ryoanji Temple is known all over the world.
3. In São Paulo, there is a mix of architecture. You can see traditional architecture in some buildings for example the Martinelli Building and the Banco do Estado de São Paulo.
4. There are also many modern buildings in São Paulo. For instance the Banco Sumitomo and Conjunto Nacional are very modern in design.
5. Bolivia offers tourists many interesting places to visit for instance the capital city of La Paz and the islands in Lake Titicaca.

**B** **Complete the sentences with *for example*, *for instance*, or *such as*. Add commas where needed. For some, there may be more than one answer.**

1. Like many big American cities, San Francisco has several ethnic neighborhoods ________________ North Beach (Italian), the Mission District (Hispanic), and Chinatown (Chinese).
2. When you visit the ethnic neighborhoods of Miami, you feel that you are in a foreign country. ________________ in Little Havana you can easily imagine that you are in Cuba.
3. Summers are much cooler in San Francisco than in Los Angeles. ________________ the average July temperature in San Francisco is about 65 degrees Fahrenheit, but it is 85 degrees Fahrenheit in Los Angeles.
4. Mexico's Yucatán Peninsula has many luxury beach resorts ________________ Cancún and Cozumel.
5. The Yucatán is full of archeological treasures ________________ the Mayan ruins at Chichén Itzá and Tulum.

## CONCLUSION SIGNALS

In addition to the conclusion signals such as *Indeed* and *To sum up* that you have already learned (see Chapter 2, page 53), you can begin a concluding sentence with *For these (two/three/four) reasons* and *Because of* ______. Notice these two patterns:

**PATTERN 1:** **For these ______ reasons,** (+ *sentence*).

**For these two reasons,** Costa Rica is a wonderful place to study if you love wildlife.

**PATTERN 2:** **Because of** (*noun phrase*), (+ *sentence*).

**Because of its diverse habitats and many animal species,** Costa Rica is a wonderful place to study if you love wildlife.

**PRACTICE 8** **Using Conclusion Signals**

**A** **Look back at the outline in Part A of Practice 5, page 145. Use *Indeed* or *To sum up*, *For these* ______ *reasons,* and *Because of* ______ to rewrite the concluding sentence in three different ways.**

1. Indeed, if you're looking for great food, amazing service, and reasonable prices, Joe's Diner is the place to go.
2. ______
3. ______

**B** **Look back at the outline in Part B of Practice 5, page 146. Write three different conclusions, using *Indeed* or *To sum up*, *For these* ______ *reasons*, and *Because of* ______.**

1. ______
2. ______
3. ______

**TRY IT OUT!** **Write a paragraph recommending a place to study English using the outline you created in Practice 1 (page 139). Follow these directions.**

1. Follow your outline as you write your draft.
2. Use transition signals to introduce your reasons and examples. Try to use *for example*, *for instance*, and *such as* at least once.
3. Add a concluding sentence. Remember to use an appropriate conclusion signal, such as *Indeed*, *To sum up*, *For* ______ *reasons*, or *Because of* ______.
4. Proofread your paragraph, and correct any mistakes.

## SENTENCE STRUCTURE

In Chapter 3, you learned about complex sentences with dependent time clauses. In this section, you will look at complex sentences with dependent reason clauses and complex sentences with dependent condition clauses.

## COMPLEX SENTENCES WITH REASON CLAUSES AND CONDITION CLAUSES

A **reason clause** is a dependent clause that explains why something happens or why someone does something. It has a subject and verb and begins with an introductory word known as a **reason subordinator**. *Because* and *since* are **reason subordinators.**

| Reason Subordinators | |
|---|---|
| **because** | They canceled the game because the field was too wet. |
| **since** | Since the field was too wet, they canceled the game. |

A **condition clause** is a dependent clause that states a condition that causes a certain result. It has a subject and verb and begins with an introductory word known as a **condition subordinator**. *If* is a condition subordinator.

| Condition Subordinator | |
|---|---|
| **if** | My best friend John is unhappy if he doesn't get an A in every class. |

Like time clauses, reason clauses and condition clauses can come before or after the independent clause. If you use a reason or condition clause before the independent clause, you must use a comma to separate the two clauses.

**Because the field was too wet,** they canceled the game.

**If he doesn't get an A in every class,** John is unhappy.

Here are some things to know about reason and condition subordinators:

- *Because* and *since* have exactly the same meaning, and there is no difference in their use.

  **Because** Tina is good at math, she decided to become an engineer.

  **Since** Tina is good at math, she decided to become an engineer.

  Tina decided to become an engineer **because** she is good at math.

  Tina decided to become an engineer **since** she is good at math.

- The word *since* can be either a reason or a time subordinator.

  **Since** I don't own a car, I take the bus to school. (REASON)

  **Since** Eddie started lifting weights, he has become much stronger. (TIME)

- *Because* is a subordinator. *Because of* is a two-word preposition.

  Hawaii is popular **because** it has beautiful beaches. (SUBORDINATOR)

  Hawaii is popular **because of** its beautiful beaches. (PREPOSITION)

- *If* introduces a condition.

Sentences with conditional clauses require special combinations of verb forms. In this chapter, you will work with examples of conditional sentences that deal with real situations in the present and future.

**If you don't practice,** you won't learn as quickly.

**If you go to Costa Rica,** you will see many unusual insects.

Don't open an email attachment **if you don't know the sender.**

**PRACTICE 9** **Analyzing Complex Sentences**

**A** **Read each sentence. Underline the independent clause once and the dependent clause twice. Draw a circle around the subordinator. Add a comma if needed.**

1. Tourists love Arizona because it has many interesting things to do.
2. Since summers are hot in Arizona the best time to go there is the spring or fall.
3. If you are interested in Native Americans you will enjoy visiting the Navajo and Hopi reservations[1] in northern Arizona.
4. You can visit a tribal fair[2] if you are lucky.
5. The Navajo call themselves a "nation" because they govern themselves.
6. Since the Navajo language is so difficult the U.S. military used it for secret messages in World War II.

[1] **reservations:** areas of land in the United States kept separate for Native Americans to live on

[2] **tribal fair:** an outdoor event where Native Americans celebrate their culture

**B** **Use your own ideas to complete the dependent clause of reason or condition in each sentence.**

1. I enjoy traveling because *I like to learn about new cultures*.
2. Since ______________________, I usually take the train.
3. I will take a special trip next year if ______________________.
4. Because New York City is very expensive, ______________________.
5. Since ______________________, I want to see as much of the world as possible.
6. I have to travel now because ______________________.

## PRACTICE 10 Editing Sentence and Punctuation Errors

**A** **Work alone or with a partner. Read the paragraph. Find the four sentence and punctuation errors. Bracket the four parts that need editing, and use a symbol from the box to identify each error. (HINT: Use each symbol once.)**

| | |
|---|---|
| *cs* **(comma splice)** | *P* **(punctuation error)** |
| *frag* **(fragment)** | *ro* **(run-on)** |

### Soccer

Soccer is truly the world's most popular sport. Since the game began in England about 150 years [ago it] (*P*) has spread to every corner of the globe. Millions of people go to soccer stadiums to watch their favorite team. While millions more watch on television. One reason for soccer's popularity may be its economy. Anyone can afford to play soccer because it doesn't require expensive equipment. Also, players can use almost any field or even a street to play the game. Soccer is the number one sport in most of the world, it is not the most popular sport in North America. Ice hockey is the favorite in Canada American football is the favorite in the United States. However, soccer has also gained new professional teams and fans in those countries.

**B** **On a separate sheet of paper, rewrite the paragraph correctly. Then compare answers with a partner. Make further corrections as needed.**

**PRACTICE 11** Combining Sentences

 Use a word from the box to combine the sentences in each group into a single simple, compound, or complex sentence. For some, there may be more than one answer.

| and | but | since | that | while |
|---|---|---|---|---|
| because | if | so | when | |

### My Love-Hate Relationship with Traveling

1. a. There are two reasons I love traveling for work.
   b. There are two reasons I hate traveling for work.
2. a. I work as a salesperson.
   b. I have to travel out of town for a week once a month.
3. a. First of all, I love traveling for work.
   b. Traveling for work allows me to meet new people.
   c. Traveling for work allows me to go to new places.
4. a. For example, I am interested in history.
   b. I try to set aside some time to visit a local historical site.
   c. I try to set aside some time to walk around the downtown area.
5. a. Second, I feel energized.
   b. I feel challenged.
   c. I am on my monthly sales trips.
6. a. On the other hand, traveling for work can be difficult.
   b. Sometimes I hate traveling for work.
7. a. The first reason is this.
   b. I don't sleep well in hotels.
8. a. I often watch TV late into the night.
   b. I can't fall asleep.
9. a. As a result, in the morning I'm very tired.
   b. By afternoon I need a nap.

10. a. The second reason I hate traveling is this.
    b. I miss my family.
11. a. Our sons are very young.
    b. They don't understand why I am away.
    c. They want to talk to me every night.
12. a. I am away for an entire week.
    b. It is hard on my sons.
    c. It is hard on my wife.
    d. It is hard on me.
13. a. I get a promotion next year.
    b. I will have a sales area closer to home.
    c. I won't have to do overnight trips.
14. a. In conclusion, I have a love-hate relationship with traveling.
    b. I try to stay positive.
    c. I try to focus on the good things.

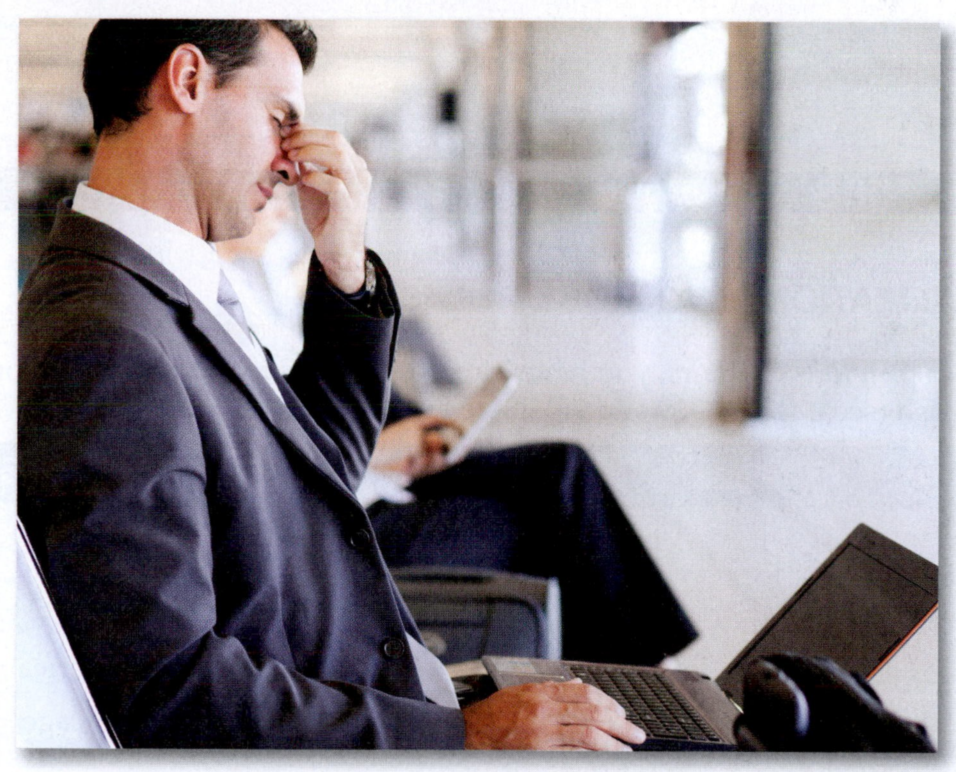

**B** Write the new sentences from Part A as a paragraph.

My Love-Hate Relationship with Traveling

There are two reasons I love traveling for work and two reasons I hate it.

## MECHANICS

### CAPITALIZATION: TWO MORE RULES

In previous chapters, you have learned ten rules for capitalizing words in English (see pages 18–19 and 96). Here are two additional rules:

| RULES | EXAMPLES |
|---|---|
| **Capitalize:** | |
| **1.** some abbreviations | IBM USA UCLA UK UAE |
| **NOTE 1:** If a name includes nouns and prepositions, only the first letter of each noun is included in the abbreviation. | United States of America = USA<br>City Colleges of Chicago = CCC |
| **NOTE 2:** Capitalize only the first letter of the abbreviation of a person's title. | Dr. Mr. Mrs. Prof. |
| **2.** all words in a greeting, but only the first word in the closing of a letter or email | Dear Sir: Love,<br>Dear Madam, Best wishes, |

## PRACTICE 12 Editing Capitalization Errors

**Work alone or with a partner. Read the email. Change the small letters to capital letters where necessary.** ***See Appendix E, page 199, to review the rules.***

dear miki,

well, here i am in new york city. i still can't believe that i'm actually here! i arrived on saturday after a long flight from paris on air france. the food was excellent, and so was the movie. we saw the new romance, *island girl*. i stayed saturday and sunday nights at the fairmont hotel near rockefeller center. then on monday i moved into my dormitory at columbia university.

i spent my entire first weekend here sightseeing. I saw many famous places: rockefeller center, the united nations, the guggenheim museum, the new york stock exchange, and the statue of liberty. i also visited another famous art museum and the nbc television studios.

today is a holiday in the united states. it is labor day, so all government offices, schools, and banks are closed. people in the usa celebrate the end of summer by having a three-day weekend. many new yorkers spend the day in central park or go to the beach on long island.

i learned some interesting things about new york. its nickname is "the big apple," but no one knows why it's called an apple and not a banana or an orange. maybe it's because the apple is the state fruit. another interesting fact is that musicians who play in the subway have to audition[1] before they get permission to perform. many of the subway musicians are extremely talented.

well, that's all for now. classes begin next week. i'm having a good time, but i miss you all, and i really miss french food. write soon.

with love,

nicole

---

[1] **audition**: give a short performance as a test of one's ability to perform

## PUNCTUATION: FOUR MORE COMMA RULES

In Chapter 3 (page 99), you learned four rules for using commas. Here are four more comma rules:

| Rules | Examples |
|---|---|
| **Use a comma:** | |
| **1.** to separate thousands, millions, billions, etc. | The trip cost them over $3,000.<br>The college has over 25,000 students. |
| **Note 1:** Do not use a comma in a number that expresses a year or is part of an address. | 2935 Main Street |
| **Note 2:** Do not use a comma to separate dollars from cents or whole numbers from decimals. Instead, use a decimal point. | $59.95 $6\frac{7}{8} = 6.875$<br>$2,999.99 4.5% |
| **2.** to separate the parts of dates and after years in the middle of a sentence | The third millennium started on January 1, 2001, not on January 1, 2000. |
| **3.** to separate the parts of a U.S. address, EXCEPT between the state and the zip code, when the address is in a sentence | The address of the Office of Admissions is 1410 NE Campus Parkway, Seattle, WA 98195. |
| **Note:** When you write an address in a letter or on an envelope, use a comma between the city and state, but do not use a comma at the end of each line. | Office of Admissions<br>1410 NE Campus Parkway<br>Seattle, WA 98195 |
| **4.** after the greeting and closing of an email or a personal letter, and after the closing of an email, a personal letter, or a business letter. | Dear Michiko, Love,<br>Dear Mom, Very truly yours, |
| **Note:** In business letters and formal emails, a colon (:) is typically used after the greeting. | Dear Ms. Prescott:<br>Dear Sir or Madam:<br>To Whom It May Concern: |

**PRACTICE 13** **Editing Commas**

 **Work alone or with a partner. Review the comma rules on pages 99 and 158. Read the paragraphs. Add commas where necessary. (Not all sentences need them.)**

**PARAGRAPH 1**

Some students work full time and go to school part time. For example, one of my classmates takes two courses and works 40 hours a week. Since he is also married and has two children he is a very busy person. He works at night attends class in the morning and sleeps when he can. When he fell asleep in class yesterday we decided not to wake him up.

**PARAGRAPH 2**

Scientists believe that animals can think feel and communicate just as humans can. My dog certainly acts like a human at times. For instance when he does something bad he looks guilty. He hangs his head drops his tail and looks up at me with sad eyes. Later we usually discover the reason for his guilty looks but it's hard to punish him.

**PARAGRAPH 3**

At the moment China is the country with the largest population but experts say that India will overtake it by the year 2040. In that year India's population will be around 1520000000 (over 1.5 billion) while China's population will only be around 1450000000 (1.4 billion).

**PARAGRAPH 4**

My mother lives in Miami in the winter and in Denver in the summer. When it becomes too hot in Florida she moves to Colorado. She moves back to Florida when it gets too cold in Colorado. Her address in Florida is P.O. Box 695 Miami FL 33167 and her address in Colorado is 3562 State Street Apt. 3-C Denver CO 80210.

*(continued on next page)*

**Paragraph 5**

On Sunday June 10 2012 I graduated from college. Then on Monday June 11 2012 I started my first full-time job. I couldn't wait to get my first paycheck but I was quickly disappointed. I was expecting over $4000 but the check was for only $3245.75. That was an important lesson. When you enter the real world you have to pay taxes.

**B** **On a separate sheet of paper, write eight sentences illustrating each of the comma rules on pages 99 and 158, but leave out the commas. Then give your sentences to a partner and ask him or her to put in the commas.**

*First of all I feel totally relaxed when I'm at the lake.*

## Applying Vocabulary: Using Nouns that Describe Geography

Before you begin your writing assignment, review what you learned about words that describe geography on pages 141–142.

### PRACTICE 14 Using Words that Describe Geography

**Work with a partner. Answer the questions.**

1. What is your favorite beach?
2. What places come to mind when you hear the word *volcano?* Do you know of any places where volcanoes have erupted recently?
3. Can you name a city or country that is famous for one or more canals?
4. Name a swamp that you have visited or that you know about. Where is it? What kinds of wildlife does it have?
5. What do you know about rainforests? List four things.
6. Would you like to live in a house on the coast? Why or why not?
7. What continent do you want to visit someday? Why?
8. Imagine you have to do a research paper about a habitat that is common in your area. Which habitat would you write about? Why?

## WRITING ASSIGNMENT

In this chapter, your assignment is to write a paragraph recommending an area to live in. It can be your hometown, the place where you live now, or any place that you know well. Give at least three reasons why a person would enjoy living there, and support your reasons with specific examples. Use the writing model about Costa Rica on page 140 as a guide.

### STEP 1: Prewrite to get ideas.

- Use listing, clustering, or freewriting to brainstorm reasons and examples.
- Study your prewriting and decide on two to four reasons to write about. Make sure you can include at least one specific example for each reason. The more examples you give, the better your paragraph will be.
- Organize your reasons and examples by making an outline. Make your outline as detailed as possible. It should be similar to the outline on page 139.
- Review the words in Looking at Vocabulary and Applying Vocabulary on pages 141–142 and 160. Look at your outline again and, if possible, add in some words to describe the geography of the place.

### STEP 2: Write the first draft.

- Write *FIRST DRAFT* at the top of your paper.
- Follow your outline to write your paragraph.
- Add transition signals to introduce your reasons and examples.
- Try to include at least three complex sentences with clauses of reason and condition.

### STEP 3: Revise and edit the first draft.

- Exchange papers with a partner, and give each other feedback on your paragraphs. Use Chapter 5 Peer Review on page 214.
- Consider your partner's feedback and revise your paragraph. Mark changes on your first draft.
- Check your paragraph carefully against Chapter 5 Writer's Self-Check on page 215, and make more changes as necessary.

**STEP 4: Write a new draft.**

- Refer to the changes you made on your first draft and do a final draft of your paragraph.
- Proofread it carefully.
- Hand it in to your teacher. Your teacher may also ask you to hand in your prewriting, your outline, and your first draft.

**SELF-ASSESSMENT**

In this chapter, you learned to:

❍ Use listing and outlining to brainstorm and organize ideas

❍ Develop a paragraph with reasons and examples

❍ Write effective conclusion sentences

❍ Use complex sentences with reason and condition clauses

❍ Apply more rules of capitalization and comma usage

❍ Write, revise, and edit a paragraph with reasons and examples

Which ones can you do well? Mark them ✓

Which ones do you need to practice more? Mark them ✗

# EXPANSION

## TIMED WRITING

To succeed in academic writing you need to be able to write quickly and fluently. For example, you might have to write a paragraph for a test in class, and you only have 30 minutes. In this activity, you will write a paragraph in class. You will have 30 minutes. To complete the activity in time, follow the directions.

1. Read the prompt below (or the prompt your teacher assigns) carefully. Make sure you understand the question or task. Then decide on the topic of your paragraph. (3 minutes)
2. Use listing to get ideas. Then read over your list and decide which ideas you will write about. Edit your list and then make an outline to organize your ideas. (8 minutes)
3. Write your paragraph. Be sure to include a title, a topic sentence, supporting ideas, transition signals for reasons and examples, and a concluding sentence. (15 minutes)

4. Proofread your paragraph. Correct any mistakes. (4 minutes)
5. Give your paper to your teacher.

**Prompt:** Write a paragraph recommending a place you can go for a day trip. Include at least three reasons why someone should visit this place. Give examples and details to support your reasons.

## YOUR JOURNAL

Continue making entries in your journal. If you cannot think of a topic for a journal entry, try one of these ideas:

- Imagine that one of your friends has asked your advice about a major purchase that he or she is about to make (for example, a car, laptop, cell phone, or camera). What would you recommend? Support your suggestion with reasons and examples.
- What type of area do you like to visit when you have free time? For example, do you prefer the mountains, a lake, or a city park? Write about why you like the area.
- What is your favorite place to shop for clothing? Explain the reasons you like it and give examples and details.

*For more ideas for journal entries, see Appendix A on page 193.*

# CHAPTER 6 EXPRESSING YOUR OPINION

## OBJECTIVES

**Writers need certain skills.**

**In this chapter, you will learn to:**

- Distinguish between facts and opinions
- Introduce reasons and examples with transition signals
- Use outlining to organize reasons and details
- Write adjective clauses with *who*, *which*, and *that*
- Identify and fix fragments
- Use quotation marks correctly
- Write, revise, and edit an opinion paragraph

*Ancient Greek philosophers enjoyed meeting in public to discuss their opinions. What techniques do you think they used to present their ideas convincingly?*

# INTRODUCTION

In the previous chapter, you learned how to write a paragraph using reasons and examples to support your ideas. In this chapter, you will learn how to organize a paragraph in which you express an **opinion** supported by details and facts. You will also learn about adjective clauses with *who, which,* and *that*.

To help you get ideas for writing, you will first do some prewriting.

# PREWRITING

In this section, you will practice using ideas from reading to support your opinion.

## GETTING IDEAS FROM READING

When you express your opinion in writing, you may support your reasons with examples and details from personal knowledge and experience. However, your writing will be stronger and more convincing if you can also include facts, ideas, and quotes from one or more other sources. These might include newspaper or magazine articles as well as information from websites and reference books.

**PRACTICE 1** **Getting Ideas from Reading**

**A** Read the blog post. Be ready to answer questions about the writer's main idea and supporting details.

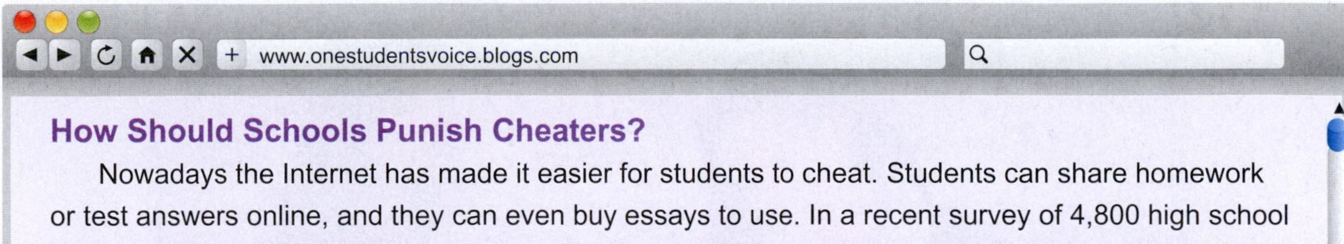

www.onestudentsvoice.blogs.com

### How Should Schools Punish Cheaters?

Nowadays the Internet has made it easier for students to cheat. Students can share homework or test answers online, and they can even buy essays to use. In a recent survey of 4,800 high school students, 53 percent admitted to cheating on tests, and 62 percent said they had turned in homework that was not their own work.

Few students are caught cheating, but when it happens, the punishment is often severe. Some schools remove the student from the class, while other schools suspend[1] or expel[2] the student. The principal usually puts a note about cheating in the student's academic record, which may become part of a student's college application file someday.

[1] **suspend:** officially stop a student from attending school because he/she has broken rules

[2] **expel:** officially make a student leave a school

*(continued on next page)*

Last week, a Westridge High School junior copied a classmate's homework in his honors math class[3]. The teacher caught him, and he admitted to cheating. Consequently, he had to withdraw from the class for the rest of the year. The student knew this might happen because the previous September he and his parents had signed an academic honesty statement for the honors class that clearly explained the teacher's cheating policy: The punishment for anyone caught cheating even one time was immediate removal from the class.

However, the student's father, who is a lawyer, wants to fight the punishment. He says that the school rules call for removal from a class after a student is caught cheating twice, not once. The father believes his son should remain in the honors class because the rules of the school and the rules of the teacher are in conflict with each other. In addition, he says the punishment is too severe for a practice that is so common among students. Removal from the honors class will make it impossible for his son to get into a top university. Yesterday, the father started legal action against the school.

The school officials are firm in their decision. "If we do not punish cheating, then we reward students who cheat and we put honest students at a disadvantage," says Ann Linsione, the principal. "Students who study long hours and work hard should not have to compete against dishonest students for top grades." Most students agree. "We are all under a lot of pressure," says one honors student. "Actually, I feel bad for the guy because he's a smart student who made a bad choice. But, in the end, there's no excuse for dishonesty."

*What's your opinion? Do you think the punishment is too harsh? Send your comments, and I will post your ideas in my next blog.*

[3] **honors math class:** a math class in which only top students attend

**B** With a partner or small group, discuss the question: Do you think the punishment is too harsh?

**C** Check (✓) the statement that best expresses your opinion. Then use the information from the blog and your own knowledge and experience to complete the outline below. Save your outline to use in the Try It Out! activity on page 177.

**DO YOU THINK THE PUNISHMENT IS TOO HARSH?**

☐ YES, it is too harsh. The student should be allowed to stay in the honors class.

☐ NO, it is not too harsh. The student should be removed from the honors class.

Outline

| | |
|---|---|
| 1ST REASON | A. |
| SUPPORTING DETAILS | 1. |
| | 2. |
| 2ND REASON | B. |
| SUPPORTING DETAILS | 1. |
| | 2. |
| 3RD REASON | C. |
| SUPPORTING DETAILS | 1. |
| | 2. |

## OPINION PARAGRAPHS

An **opinion** is a statement of someone's belief. When you say, "I believe . . ." or "I think that . . . ," you are expressing an opinion. In everyday life, people talk and write about their opinion or point of view on a wide variety of issues. Examples include: Should smoking be allowed everywhere? Do you agree with restrictions on teenagers during their first year of driving? Should the government ban the sale of handguns?

If you look at the "Letters to the Editor" section of any newspaper, you will find letters from people discussing their points of view. People post their opinions on online news sites and in blogs. In college classes, you often have to express and support your opinions.

Here are four keys to writing a successful opinion paragraph:

- State your opinion clearly in the topic sentence.
- Present the reasons for your opinion in logical order.
- Use facts to support each reason.
- End with a powerful concluding sentence that your reader will remember.

## LOOKING AT THE MODEL

The writing model contains one writer's opinion about video games.

**Work with a partner or in a small group. Read the model. Then answer the questions.**

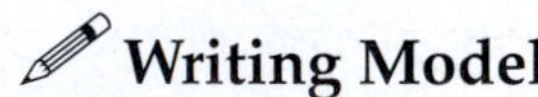

**Writing Model**

### Video Games and Violence

In my opinion, violent video games are harmful to young people. First of all, studies show that playing these games can cause changes in the behavior of young people. According to researchers, immediately after playing these games, young people have more aggressive thoughts and angry feelings. In addition, frequent players get into more fights at school and have more arguments with their teachers. A second reason that violent video games are harmful to young people is that, in my opinion, they make young people less sensitive to violence in the real world. I believe that these games make it entertaining to shoot and kill, and the line between imaginary violence and real violence becomes very thin or disappears entirely for children. Thirteen-year-old Noah Wilson, for example, was stabbed to death by a friend who often played the violent game *Mortal Kombat*. On a talk show that I watched recently, Noah's mother claimed that the boy who stabbed her son was acting out the part of Cyrex, a character in the game. A third reason is that, in my opinion, children who do not have good home situations or who have emotional problems may not understand that violence is not a good solution. An extreme example of this kind of thinking resulted in the Columbine High School massacre[1] in 1999. Two students shot and killed 12 classmates, a teacher, and themselves at the Colorado high school. The two young killers were fans of the video games *Doom* and *Wolfenstein 3D*. For these three reasons, I feel that violent video games are harmful to young people and should be controlled—or, even better, banned[2].

**Sources:**

1. Jill U. Adams, "Effects of violent video games," the *Los Angeles Times*, May 3, 2010, articles.latimes.com/2010/may/03/health/la-he-closer-20100503 (accessed July 1, 2012).
2. Paraphrase from a transcript of the television program *Donahue*, July 22, 2002, lionlamb.org/news_articles/donahue_july_22.htm (accessed November 3, 2006).

[1] **massacre:** murder of many people
[2] **banned:** prohibited, not allowed

## Questions about the Model

1. What is the writer's opinion about violent video games? What phrase does he use to introduce his opinion?
2. How many reasons does the writer give for his opinion?
3. What transition signals does the writer use to introduce his reasons?
4. In your opinion, which reason is stronger: the first one or the last one? Why?

## Looking at Vocabulary: Word Forms

Learning word forms is a good way to expand your vocabulary and add more variety to your writing. For example, if you know both the noun and adjective forms of a word, you can avoid repeating the same words over and over.

> A second reason that **violent** video games are harmful to young people is that, in my opinion, they make young people less sensitive to **violence** in the real world.

## PRACTICE 2 Looking at Word Forms

**A** Look at the writing model. Find and underline the adjective forms of the nouns in the first column. Then write the adjectives you found in the second column.

| Nouns | Adjectives |
|---|---|
| 1. violence | violent |
| 2. harm | __________ |
| 3. aggression | __________ |
| 4. anger | __________ |
| 5. sensitivity | __________ |
| 6. entertainment | __________ |
| 7. imagination | __________ |
| 8. emotion | __________ |

**B** Circle the correct word form that completes each sentence.

1. Some parents disapprove of video games that promote *(violence / violent)*.
2. They are afraid that such games do more *(harm / harmful)* than good.
3. Video games are a popular form of *(entertainment / entertaining)* for many people.
4. Some people believe that children show more *(aggression / aggressive)* after playing violent video games.
5. During the last part of the movie, my friend became very *(emotion / emotional)* and began to cry.
6. Since he was a child, the artist has always had a wild *(imagination / imaginative)*.
7. I didn't think that the TV show was very *(entertainment / entertaining)*.
8. Clara has a great *(sensitivity / sensitive)* for animals. She seems to understand them very well.

## ORGANIZATION

In this section, you will look at how to organize an opinion paragraph. You will also learn how to introduce your reasons and supporting examples with appropriate transition signals.

### FACTS AND OPINIONS

An **opinion** is what someone believes. People can disagree with opinions. A **fact**, however, is a true statement that no one can disagree with.

Read these sentence pairs. Which ones are facts, and which ones are opinions?

| | |
|---|---|
| The sun rises in the east. | The sunrise was beautiful this morning. |
| The temperature of the lake is 55 degrees Fahrenheit. | The lake is too cold for swimming. |
| According to highway accident reports, using a cell phone while driving is dangerous. | Using a cell phone while driving is dangerous. |
| Women could not vote in the United States until 1920. | Everyone should vote. |
| Mrs. King said, "I am a good mother." | Mrs. King is a good mother. |

The sentences in the left column are facts. They are true. Even the last sentence, "Mrs. King said, 'I am a good mother,'" is a fact. It is true that she said that. What she said—"I am a good mother"—is an opinion. However, a statement that reports what she said is a fact because no one can disagree that she said it.

The sentences in the right column are opinions. People can disagree with them. They may or may not be true.

Of course, you can use opinions as reasons, but your paragraph will be stronger and more convincing if you support your opinion with facts.

**PRACTICE 3** **Identifying Facts and Opinions**

Complete the outline for the writing model on pages 168–169. Use full sentences, but do not include transition signals. Then analyze each sentence in the column on the right. Write *F* for fact and *O* for opinion.

Video Games and Violence

| | | |
|---|---|---|
| TOPIC SENTENCE | In my opinion, violent video games are harmful to young people. | O |
| 1ST REASON | A. Studies show that playing these games can cause changes in the behavior of young people. | F |
| SUPPORTING DETAILS | 1. According to researchers, immediately after playing these games, players have more aggressive thoughts and angry feelings. | ______ |
| | 2. Frequent players get into more fights at school and have more arguments with their teachers. | ______ |
| 2ND REASON | B. In my opinion, they make young people less sensitive to violence. | ______ |
| SUPPORTING DETAILS | 1. ______________________________ | ______ |
| | 2. Noah Wilson (13) was stabbed to death by a friend who often played the violent game *Mortal Kombat*. | ______ |
| | 3. On a talk show I watched recently, Noah's mother claimed that the boy who stabbed her son was acting out the part of Cyrex, a character in *Mortal Kombat*. | ______ |
| 3RD REASON | C. ______________________________ | ______ |
| SUPPORTING DETAILS | 1. An extreme example of this thinking resulted in the Columbine High School massacre in 1999. | ______ |
| | 2. ______________________________ | ______ |
| | 3. The two young killers were fans of the video games *Doom* and *Wolfenstein 3D*. | ______ |
| CONCLUDING SENTENCE | ______________________________ | ______ |

## TRANSITION SIGNALS IN OPINION PARAGRAPHS

Here are some things to keep in mind about transition signals in opinion paragraphs:

- When you state an opinion, you should indicate that it is an opinion by using an opinion signal, such as one of these:

| OPINION SIGNALS | EXAMPLES |
|---|---|
| In my opinion, . . . (*with a comma*) | In my opinion, everyone should be allowed to own a gun. |
| In my view, . . . (*with a comma*) | In my view, no one should be allowed to own a gun. |
| I believe (that) . . . (*without a comma*) | I believe that smoking should not be allowed in public places. |
| I think (that) . . . (*without a comma*) | I think smokers have rights, too. |

- To give information from an outside source (a book, a newspaper, another person), use *according to* with a comma.

| SOURCE SIGNAL | EXAMPLES |
|---|---|
| According to X, . . . (*with a comma*) | According to Gregory, his mother never wrote to him or sent him birthday cards. |
| | According to a story in *Science Today* magazine, the Earth is becoming warmer. |

- In your concluding sentence, you can remind your reader of the number of reasons.

| CONCLUSION SIGNAL | EXAMPLE |
|---|---|
| For these (two, three, four, and so on) reasons, . . . (*with a comma*) | For these three reasons, I believe that violent video games are harmful to young people. |

If you wish, you can also add a recommendation for action.

For these three reasons, I believe that violent video games are harmful to young people and should be controlled—or, even better, banned.

## PRACTICE 4 Outlining an Opinion Paragraph

**Work alone or with a partner. Use the completed outline for Topic 1 as an example. Choose two of the remaining topics and complete the outline for each. Follow the directions.**

1. On the first line, write a topic sentence with an opinion signal.
2. Think of two or three reasons for your opinion and write them on the appropriate lines. You can write sentences or notes.
3. Think of one or more supporting details for each reason, and write them on the appropriate lines. For example, you might use:
   - statistics from a class survey that you conduct
   - a quotation from a classmate or neighbor
   - an example from personal experience
4. Write a concluding sentence that mentions the number of reasons or make a recommendation for action.

### TOPIC 1: GUN CONTROL LAWS

| | Gun Control Laws |
|---|---|
| TOPIC SENTENCE | In my opinion, responsible people should be allowed to own a gun. |
| 1ST REASON | A. People need to defend themselves in today's violent society. |
| SUPPORTING DETAILS | 1. Personal story? News story? |
| | 2. Interview classmates/neighbors to get quotations? |
| 2ND REASON | B. Criminals will always find ways to get guns. |
| SUPPORTING DETAILS | 1. Bumper sticker: "If guns are outlawed, only outlaws will have guns." |
| | 2. Statistics on crimes with guns that are not properly registered |
| 3RD REASON | C. The U.S. Bill of Rights[1] gives citizens the right to own guns. |
| SUPPORTING DETAILS | 1. Quotation from the Bill of Rights |
| | 2. Public support for legal gun possession |
| CONCLUDING SENTENCE | For these reasons, I believe laws prohibiting gun ownership are wrong. |

[1] **U.S. Bill of Rights:** the first ten amendments to the U.S. Constitution, which state the basic rights of U.S. citizens

## Topic 2: Capital Punishment[1]

Capital Punishment

TOPIC SENTENCE

1ST REASON A.

SUPPORTING DETAILS 1.

2.

2ND REASON B.

SUPPORTING DETAILS 1.

2.

3RD REASON C.

SUPPORTING DETAILS 1.

2.

CONCLUDING SENTENCE

[1] **capital punishment:** the death penalty for the most serious crimes

## Topic 3: Using Cell Phones in Public Places

Using Cell Phones in Public Places

TOPIC SENTENCE

1ST REASON A.

SUPPORTING DETAILS 1.

2.

2ND REASON B.

SUPPORTING DETAILS 1.

2.

3RD REASON C.

SUPPORTING DETAILS 1.

2.

CONCLUDING SENTENCE

### TOPIC 4: YOUR OWN IDEA

TITLE

TOPIC SENTENCE

1ST REASON A.

SUPPORTING DETAILS 1.

2.

2ND REASON B.

SUPPORTING DETAILS 1.

2.

3RD REASON C.

SUPPORTING DETAILS 1.

2.

CONCLUDING SENTENCE

**TRY IT OUT!** **Review the blog post about cheating on pages 165–166 and the outline you completed in Practice 1C on page 167. On a separate sheet of paper, write an opinion paragraph on this question: Do you think the punishment is too harsh? Follow these directions.**

1. Organize your ideas about the question into an outline. Remember to add a topic sentence and a concluding sentence.
2. Follow your outline as you write your draft.
3. Use transition signals where appropriate.
4. Proofread your paragraph and correct any mistakes.

## SENTENCE STRUCTURE

In the previous chapters, you learned about different types of dependent clauses, including time, reason, and condition clauses. In this section, you will learn about another kind of dependent clause called an **adjective clause**.

### ADJECTIVE CLAUSES WITH *WHO, WHICH,* AND *THAT*

Adjective clauses (also called relative clauses) begin with words such as *who*, *which*, and *that*. These dependent clauses act like adjectives because they give more information about a noun.

Here are some things to know about adjective clauses:

- Adjective clauses begin with the words *who, which*, and *that* (among others).

  *who* is used for people

  *which* is used for things

  *that* is used for things (and for people in informal English)

- An adjective clause follows the noun it gives more information about.
- Commas are sometimes used with adjective clauses, and sometimes not. (You will learn about this on page 180.)

In the examples, the adjective clause is highlighted. An arrow points to the noun that the adjective clause gives more information about.

If we do not punish cheating, then we reward students **who cheat**.

The principal usually puts a note about cheating in the student's academic record, **which may be part of a student's college application file someday**.

Sixty-two percent turned in homework **that was done by someone else**.

**PRACTICE 5** **Identifying Adjective Clauses**

**Look at each sentence. Underline the adjective clauses twice, and circle *who*, *which*, or *that*. Then draw an arrow back to the noun that the adjective clause gives more information about.**

1. In my opinion, students who wear uniforms behave better.
2. Long Beach, California, which was one of the first cities in the United States to require uniforms in elementary and middle school, reported increased attendance and decreased bad behavior.

3. According to a survey that was done in South Carolina, middle school students who wear school uniforms have more positive feelings about their schools than students in schools that do not require uniforms.

4. Schools that require uniforms help lessen economic and social differences among students.

5. Students who cannot afford the latest fashions do not feel self-conscious.

6. Physical appearance, which can cause middle school students much anxiety, is less important when everyone wears the same uniform.

**PRACTICE 6** **Adjective Clauses with *Who* and *Which***

**Complete the adjective clause in each sentence with *who* or *which*. (Do not use *that* in this exercise.)**

1. In arranged marriages, ____which____ are common in many countries, someone else chooses your marriage partner.

2. Sometimes the parents, ________________ know their child better than anyone, choose.

3. Sometimes the parents hire a matchmaker, ________________ charges a fee to find the right person.

4. The two young people are probably very nervous at their first meeting, ________________ usually takes place in the bride's home.

5. In some cultures, a young man or woman ________________ doesn't like the parents' or matchmaker's choice may say no.

6. Marrying for love, ________________ is the custom in most Western cultures, does not guarantee happiness.

7. The divorce rate among couples ________________ marry for love is very high.

8. People ________________ listened only to their hearts sometimes wish they had listened to their heads.

## PUNCTUATING ADJECTIVE CLAUSES

Using commas around an adjective clause depends on whether the clause provides extra information about the noun or whether it provides information that is necessary to identify the noun.

Compare these sentences:

| EXTRA INFORMATION (USE COMMAS) | NECESSARY INFORMATION (DO NOT USE COMMAS) |
| --- | --- |
| Rachel Moore, **who never votes in elections**, is not a good citizen. | A person **who never votes in elections** is not a good citizen. |

In the sentence on the left, the adjective clause *who never votes in elections* provides extra information about Rachel Moore. You don't need this information to identify her because her name tells us who she is. If an adjective clause gives extra information, separate it from the rest of the sentence with commas.

In the sentence on the right, the adjective clause *never votes in elections* provides information that is necessary to identify *person*. What kind of person is not a good citizen?—A person who never votes in elections. If the information in an adjective clause is necessary, do not use commas.

Here are additional examples.

| EXTRA INFORMATION (USE COMMAS) | NECESSARY INFORMATION (DO NOT USE COMMAS) |
| --- | --- |
| Children shouldn't play the video game Grand Theft Auto, **which teaches criminal behavior**. | Children shouldn't play video games **that teach criminal behavior**. |
| Sergio, **who is sitting next to the window**, isn't paying attention. | The student **who is sitting next to the window** isn't paying attention. |
| Let's study at my apartment, **which is just a few minutes from campus**. | They rented an apartment **that was just a few minutes from campus**. |

**Writing Tip**

Use *that* (not *which*) with clauses that provide necessary information.

CORRECT: A college major that is very popular these days is psychology.

INCORRECT: A college major, which is very popular these days, is psychology.

Never use commas when a clause begins with *that*.

CORRECT: A book that gives synonyms for words is called a thesaurus.

INCORRECT: A book, that gives synonyms for words, is called a thesaurus.

## PRACTICE 7 Punctuating Adjective Clauses

**A** **Look at each sentence. Underline the adjective clause twice, and circle *who*, *which*, or *that*. Draw an arrow to the noun that it gives more information about. Add commas if needed.**

1. A country that has a king or queen is called a monarchy.
2. England which has a queen is a monarchy.
3. A pediatrician is a doctor who takes care of children.
4. Dr. Jones who is our neighbor is a pediatrician.
5. Students who studied got As on the final exam.
6. Gabriela and Trinh who studied together got As on the final exam.
7. My birthday is next Monday which is a holiday.
8. A holiday that is especially fun for children is Halloween.

**B** **Read the paragraph. Add commas where needed.**

### The Story of Coca-Cola

A popular beverage that is sold all over the world is Coca-Cola. A doctor who lived in Atlanta, Georgia, invented it in 1886. Dr. John Pemberton who was also a pharmacist first sold Coca-Cola as a nerve tonic[1], stimulant[2], and headache medicine. The name of the dark brown syrup that made people feel better was "Pemberton's French Wine Coca." Later someone added soda water to the syrup and it became the beverage that is our modern Coca-Cola. The first part of the name (*coca*) comes from *cocaine* which was one of the original ingredients. The second part of the name (*cola*) comes from *kola nut* which is still an ingredient today. The original formula has changed over the years. Of course, Coca-Cola no longer contains cocaine which is an illegal drug but it still tastes delicious. The formula for Coca-Cola is a secret that is carefully guarded.

---

[1] **tonic:** something that gives you energy

[2] **stimulant:** something that stimulates, gives you energy (similar to *tonic*)

## COMPLEX SENTENCES WITH ADJECTIVE CLAUSES

In this section, you will practice writing complex sentences with adjective clauses. Remember that an adjective clause is a dependent clause. Therefore, you must combine it with an independent clause to make a complex sentence.

### PRACTICE 8 Combining Clauses and Sentences

**A** Combine each independent clause on the left with an adjective clause on the right to make a complex sentence. For some, there may be more than one answer. Put the adjective clause directly after the noun it gives more information about. Add commas if needed.

| INDEPENDENT CLAUSES | ADJECTIVE CLAUSES |
| --- | --- |
| **1.** They gave their boss a Rolex watch. | **a.** who owns a yacht and a jet |
| **2.** The purse is hers. | **b.** which has a view of Central Park |
| **3.** Alice moved to New York last month. | **c.** who was celebrating his 50th birthday |
| **4.** She is living in an apartment. | **d.** who has love |
| **5.** Uncle John is a billionaire. | **e.** that is lying under the chair |
| **6.** A person has everything. | **f.** who is my best friend |

1. They gave their boss, who was celebrating his 50th birthday, a Rolex watch.

2. ______

3. ______

4. ______

5. ______

6. ______

**B** Combine each pair of simple sentences into a complex sentence containing an adjective clause with *who*, *which*, or *that*. Add commas where needed.

### Cultures in Conflict

1. Jamila Haddad ran away from home last week. Jamila is a high school student in Chicago.

   *Jamila Haddad, who is a high school student in Chicago, ran away from home last week.*

2. She ran away to avoid a marriage. The marriage was arranged by her parents.

   *She ran away to avoid a marriage that was arranged by her parents.*

3. Mr. and Mrs. Haddad are very traditional. Mr. and Mrs. Haddad are from Lebanon.

4. Jamila is the oldest daughter in the Haddad family. The Haddad family immigrated to this country seven years ago.

5. Her parents want her to marry a man. The man is 32 years old.

6. The husband-to-be lives in Lebanon. Lebanon is a country in the Middle East.

7. He owns a business. The business is very successful.

*(continued on next page)*

8. People say he is very nice. People know him.

9. Jamila ran away from home rather than marry the man. Jamila wants to go to college in her new country.

10. Mr. and Mrs. Haddad don't understand why she ran away. Mr. and Mrs. Haddad thought they had arranged a good future for their daughter.

**PRACTICE 9** **Using Adjective Clauses in Definitions**

**For items 1–5, unscramble each set of words to make a definition that contains an adjective clause. (If you need to, look up unfamiliar words in a dictionary.)**

1. A fanatic / who / a / person / extreme ideas / has / is

   A fanatic is a person who has extreme ideas.

2. A vegetarian / person / doesn't eat / meat / is / a / who

3. A hybrid / car / gasoline / and / that / a / is / runs / on / electricity

4. Transients / have / who / people / no / permanent home / are

5. The giant panda / animal / is / that / near / extinction / an / is

**For 6 and 7, write your own definitions using the words given and others as necessary.**

6. Los Angeles / city / famous for

7. Dental hygienists / people / teeth

## MORE ABOUT FRAGMENTS

In Chapter 3, you learned about the sentence error called a fragment. Sometimes this error happens when you write a dependent clause and forget to add an independent clause:

INCORRECT: If you want to transfer to a four-year college.

INCORRECT: Because it was raining when we left.

Here is another kind of sentence fragment:

INCORRECT: Ron, who also takes night classes.

INCORRECT: The book that was on the table.

This kind of fragment has no independent clause. It consists of a noun and an adjective clause.

There are two ways to correct this error:

- Finish the independent clause.

CORRECTED: Ron, who also takes night classes, ^ is very busy.

CORRECTED: The book that was on the table ^ belongs to the teacher.

- Delete *who, which*, or *that* to make a simple sentence.

CORRECTED: Ron takes night classes.

CORRECTED: The book was on the table.

**Writing Tip**

When you fix a fragment by deleting *who*, *which*, or *that*, be sure the remaining words make a meaningful sentence.

For example, take the fragment *Pedestrians who cross the street.* If you delete *who*, you get *Pedestrians cross the street.* This is not a very interesting or meaningful sentence. It is better to correct this fragment by finishing the independent clause:

Pedestrians who cross the street ^ should look in both directions before stepping off the curb.

## PRACTICE 10 Identifying Fragments

**A** Read each item. Write *F* for fragment and *S* for sentence.

F 1. Women who work.

S 2. Nowadays, more women work in traditionally male occupations.

_____ 3. For example, the field of medicine.

_____ 4. There are now more women than men in medical schools.

_____ 5. Medical schools, which didn't use to accept many women.

_____ 6. Men are also working in traditionally female occupations.

_____ 7. Such as nursing, which used to be a woman's profession.

_____ 8. More women are applying to engineering schools, too.

_____ 9. I know a young woman who is studying construction management.

_____ 10. Her dream, which is to supervise the construction of bridges and dams.

**B** On a separate sheet of paper, correct each of the fragments in Part A by completing the independent clause or by deleting *who*, *which*, or *that*.

1. Women who work have many opportunities these days.

## PRACTICE 11 Editing Fragments

**A** Work alone or with a partner. The paragraph contains several fragments. Put brackets around each one, and write *frag* above it.

**Should Schools Ban Religious Head Coverings?**

In my opinion, schools should not ban religious head coverings in school. The most important reason is freedom of religion. [Which is guaranteed by the First Amendment of the U.S. Constitution.] Many religions have special clothing and symbols. Such as turbans, headscarves, and crosses. For example, men who are followers of the Sikh religion. They must wear turbans to cover their hair. Muslim women may choose to wear scarves on their heads for religious reasons. Some Christians, both men and women, like to wear crosses on chains around their necks. It is their right to follow their beliefs, so it is wrong for a school to take away that right. A second reason is discrimination. Which is also against the law. If a school bans only head coverings. This is discrimination. Schools must also ban stars of David, crosses, and any other religious items if they ban head coverings. To sum up, banning religious head coverings is wrong. Because it violates the law that guarantees freedom of religion and because it discriminates against one group of people.

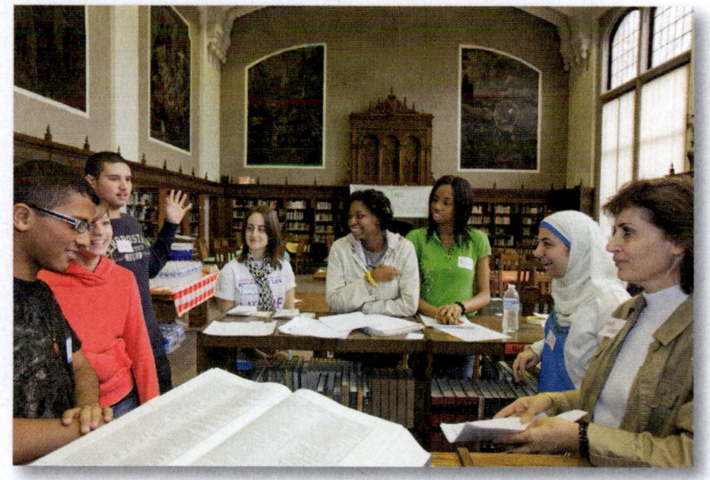

**B** Write the corrected sentence fragments on a separate sheet of paper. (HINT: Most of the errors you found can be fixed by combining the fragment with the sentence before or after it.)

The most important reason is freedom of religion, which is guaranteed by the First Amendment of the U.S. Constitution. *(Answer combines sentences 2 and 3.)*

## MECHANICS

### QUOTATION MARKS

In the opinion paragraph that you will write at the end of this chapter, you may want to use quotations from classmates you have interviewed. This section covers the rules for punctuating quotations correctly.

| Rules | Examples |
|---|---|
| **1.** Put quotation marks before and after another person's exact words. | Classmate Sabrina Reyes says, "Mothers of young children should not work because young children need their mothers at home." |
| **2.** Use a reporting phrase, such as *he says* or *she stated*. The reporting phrase can come before, after, or in the middle of the quotation. Separate it with a comma (or two commas).<br>Another useful reporting phrase is *according to* (+ name or noun). If you use someone's exact words with *according to*, use quotation marks. | **She stated**, "It's not easy to be a single mother."<br>"It's not easy," **she stated**, "to be a single mother."<br>"It's not easy to be a single mother," **she stated**.<br>**According to** classmate Sabrina Reyes, "Mothers of young children should not work because young children need their mothers at home." |
| **3.** Begin each quotation with a capital letter. When a quoted sentence is separated into two parts by a reporting phrase, begin the second part with a small letter. | "It's not easy," she stated, "to be a single mother." |
| **4.** Periods, commas, question marks, and exclamation points go inside the end quotation mark. | She said, "Goodbye."<br>"Don't leave so soon," he replied.<br>"Why shouldn't I?" she asked.<br>"Look over there!" he exclaimed. |

**PRACTICE 12** **Punctuating Quotations**

Add quotation marks, commas, capital letters, periods, and question marks as needed.

1. Before I came to the United States, my parents said to me, "Don't ~~don't~~ get sick while you are there."
2. Why not I asked

3. Medical care in the United States is very expensive they answered

4. According to a booklet about health care in the United States a two-hour visit to the emergency room can cost more than $3,000 (*not the exact words*)

5. I asked what happens if I can't pay

6. I don't know my father replied but I think you should find out

7. According to the booklet the school will provide medical insurance while you are a student (*exact words*)

8. My advisor said it doesn't cover everything, so you might want to buy additional insurance from a private company

## Applying Vocabulary: Using Word Forms

Before you begin your writing assignment, review the nouns and their equivalent adjective forms on pages 169–170.

**PRACTICE 13** **Using Word Forms**

**Discuss the questions with a partner. Try to use both the underlined word and its noun or adjective counterpart in your answer.**

1. Do you like to watch violent movies? Why or why not?

   *I don't like violent movies at all. I think they send people (and especially children) the wrong signal. The world would be a better place if people realized that they can't solve their problems with violence.*

2. Do you think that computer games are good entertainment for children? Why or why not?

3. Can you describe a person that you know that has a hard time controlling his or her anger?

4. Can you think of three situations when it is good to be a little bit aggressive?

5. Should a parent be concerned about a child who has an imaginary friend? Why or why not?

6. Do you think that some people are too sensitive? Describe someone you know who is easily hurt or offended by other people.

7. In your opinion, what human activity causes the most harm to the environment?

8. Some people think men have more control over their emotions than women. Do you think this is true?

## WRITING ASSIGNMENT

Write an opinion paragraph about one of the topics from Practice 4 on pages 174–177. Back up your opinions with at least three reasons and supporting details. Follow the steps in the writing process.

### STEP 1: Prewrite to get ideas.

- You have already outlined some ideas for two of the topics in Practice 4. Choose one topic to write about. Your teacher may suggest that you interview classmates or take a class survey to get quotations and/or statistics to use as supporting details in your paragraph.
- Add at least one quote and two or three more details to your outline.
- Review the words in Looking at Vocabulary and Applying Vocabulary on pages 169–170 and 189. Look at your outline again and, if possible, add in some of these (or similar) words.

### STEP 2: Write the first draft.

- Write *FIRST DRAFT* at the top of your paper.
- Follow your outline to write your paragraph.
- Add transition signals where appropriate.
- Try to include at least two sentences with adjective clauses.
- Use at least one quotation. Introduce the quotation with a reporting phrase, and use quotation marks as needed.

### STEP 3: Revise and edit the first draft.

- Exchange papers with a partner, and give each other feedback on your paragraphs. Use Chapter 6 Peer Review on page 216.
- Consider your partner's feedback, and revise your paragraph. Mark changes on your first draft.
- Check your paragraph carefully against Chapter 6 Writer's Self-Check on page 217, and make more changes as necessary.

### STEP 4: Write a new draft.

- Refer to the changes you made on your first draft, and do a final draft of your paragraph.
- Proofread it carefully.
- Hand it in to your teacher. Your teacher may also ask you to hand in your prewriting, your outline, and your first draft.

## SELF-ASSESSMENT

In this chapter, you learned to:

- ❍ Distinguish between facts and opinions
- ❍ Introduce reasons and examples with transition signals
- ❍ Use outlining to organize reasons and details
- ❍ Write adjective clauses with *who, which,* and *that*
- ❍ Identify and fix fragments
- ❍ Use quotation marks correctly
- ❍ Write, revise, and edit an opinion paragraph

Which ones can you do well? Mark them ✓

Which ones do you need to practice more? Mark them ✗

# EXPANSION

## TIMED WRITING

To succeed in academic writing you need to be able to write quickly and fluently. For example, you might have to write a paragraph for a test in class, and you only have 30 minutes. In this activity, you will write a paragraph in class. You will have 30 minutes. To complete the activity in time, follow the directions.

1. Read the prompt below (or the prompt your teacher assigns) carefully. Make sure you understand the question or task. Then decide on the topic of your paragraph. (3 minutes)
2. Use listing to get ideas for the reasons you will use to support your opinion. Then list details to support your reasons. You can include quotes and facts from your own experience. Edit your list, and then make an outline to organize your ideas. (8 minutes)
3. Write your paragraph. Be sure to include a title, a topic sentence, supporting ideas, transition signals, and a concluding sentence. (15 minutes)
4. Proofread your paragraph. Correct any mistakes. (4 minutes)
5. Give your paper to your teacher.

**Prompt:** In your opinion, what should the punishment be for cheating on a final test in your English class?

## YOUR JOURNAL

Continue making entries in your journal. If you cannot think of a topic for a journal entry, try one of these ideas:

- Do you think that parents should restrict how much time a 13-year-old student spends on the computer each day?
- Scientists have shown that second-hand smoke causes serious health problems. Should parents who smoke be prohibited from smoking when their children are present?
- Plastic shopping bags are very bad for the environment. They do not break down naturally in landfills and they are dangerous to animals. Some cities want to ban the use of plastic shopping bags and require stores to charge ten cents each for paper shopping bags. Do you agree or disagree with this solution?

*For more ideas for journal entries, see Appendix A on page 193.*

# APPENDICES

## APPENDIX A MORE IDEAS FOR JOURNAL WRITING

At the end of each chapter, there are several topic suggestions for writing in your journal. Here are some more ideas for journal writing.

1. Write about a special skill that you have.
2. Do you have a hobby? Explain how to do it.
3. What are your reasons for studying English? Do you need it for your job or school?
4. What is the most difficult part of learning English for you?
5. What is your favorite sport to play or watch? Why do you like it so much? Give reasons and examples.
6. Describe the appearance and personality of one of your friends. What do you like best about this person?
7. Write about an American custom that you like or dislike. Describe the custom. Support your opinion with reasons and examples.
8. Think of an important story in the news. Describe what happened. Then write about how the event makes you feel.
9. What do you think you will be doing in twenty years? Describe what you think your life will be like.
10. Write a paragraph about a big mistake you once made. What did you learn from the experience?
11. What do you think is the right age to get married? Why?
12. What qualities make a good friend?
13. What role do electronic devices like computers and mobile phones play in your life? Which device is most important to you? Why?
14. Write a paragraph about your favorite food. How do you make it? Why do you like it so much?
15. What do you think is the best car to own? Why?
16. Write a paragraph about a movie star or singer you like. What qualities do you find special about this person?
17. Discuss a belief that you have or used to have.
18. Write a paragraph about an event from your childhood.
19. Describe a favorite possession. Why do you like it so much?
20. What role does music play in your life? What kind do you like to listen to most? Give reasons for your answer.
21. What is the most special gift you have ever given or received? What made it so special?
22. Describe a special day or event in your life. Why was it important to you?
23. Write a paragraph about a frightening or funny experience you have had.
24. What was the best vacation you ever took? What did you do and see? Why was it such a good experience?
25. Describe a place that is special to you. What memories do you have of it? What special meaning does it have for you?

| Term | Definition / Function | Examples |
|---|---|---|
| **Action verb**<br>*Also see the entries for* Linking Verb *and* Verb *below.* | a verb that expresses an action such as *hit*, *live*, *lose*, *speak*, *go*, or *come* | I **lost** my keys.<br>He **lives** in Rome now. |
| **Adjective** | a word that describes a noun or pronoun | I have a **new** neighbor named Eva.<br>Eva has a **nice** smile.<br>She is **friendly**. |
| **Adverb** | a word that describes a verb, an adjective, another adverb, or a complete sentence, often to tell how, when, or where | The actors talked **fast**.<br>It was **really** difficult to understand them.<br>I listened **very** carefully.<br>I'm going to watch the same movie **tomorrow**.<br>Meet me **here** at 9:00. |
| **Article** | the word *a*, *an*, or *the*, used to introduce a noun | There is **a** café on Green Street.<br>**The** café is called Java's.<br>It is **an** interesting place. |
| **Clause** | a group of related words that has a subject and a verb | This is my book.<br>. . . because it was late. |
| **Coordinating conjunction** | a word that connects equal elements in a sentence (*for*, *and*, *nor*, *but*, *or*, *yet*, and *so*) | It is my birthday, **so** I want to celebrate.<br>I know I'm on a diet, **but** let's have cake **and** ice cream. |
| **Dependent clause** | a clause that cannot be a complete sentence | After I got up, . . .<br>because it was late. |
| **Gerund** | a verb ending in *-ing* that is used as a noun | **Dancing** is fun.<br>I am sad about **leaving**. |
| **Independent clause** | a clause that is, or could be, a complete sentence | **I took a shower**.<br>After I got up, **I took a shower**. |
| **Linking verb**<br>*Also see the entries for* Action Verb *above and for* Verb *below.* | a verb that connects the subject to information about the subject | She **is** in a band.<br>I **am** his boss. |

| TERM | DEFINITION / FUNCTION | EXAMPLES |
| --- | --- | --- |
| **Noun** | a word that names a person, place, or thing and that can be used as a subject or an object | I have a **roommate** at **school**.<br>His **name** is **Mark**.<br>He is from **Hong Kong**.<br>**Mark** and I like the same **music**. |
| **Noun phrase** | a group of words ending with a noun that belong together in meaning | He lives in **that old house** on **the corner**.<br>I'm reading **a really good book**. |
| **Object** | a noun, noun phrase, object pronoun, or possessive pronoun that receives the action of certain verbs | Mark is always losing **things**.<br>Today he lost **his keys**.<br>His girlfriend found **them**.<br>I saw **mine** on the table. |
| **Phrase** | a group of related words that does not have both a subject and a verb | I had **a frightening experience**.<br>It happened **a few days ago**. |
| **Preposition** | a word that shows direction, location, ownership, and so on | I went **into** my room and looked **under** the bed.<br>Juan is **from** Guadalupe **in** Mexico. |
| **Prepositional phrase** | a preposition plus a noun, pronoun, or gerund | The train left **at noon**. Hundreds of people were **on it**. |
| **Pronoun** | a word that replaces a noun | Ed knew where the pen was.<br>**He** had hidden **it**. |
| **Subject** | a noun, noun phrase, or subject pronoun that tells who or what the sentence is about | **Mark** rarely loses his keys.<br>**His sister** lives in Boston.<br>**She** has a nice house. |
| **Subordinating conjunction ("subordinator")** | a word or phrase that introduces a dependent clause | **When** it's hot, we go to the beach.<br>He couldn't find the file **because** he lost it. |
| **Verb** | a word or group of words that expresses an action, feeling, or state | Davina **plays** the guitar and **sings**.<br>He **feels** happy today.<br>She **enjoyed** the opera. |

# APPENDIX C SENTENCE TYPES

There are three basic types of sentences: **simple**, **compound**, and **complex**.

## Simple Sentences

A simple sentence is a sentence with one independent clause.

It's hot today.

John and Mary are engaged to be married.

I go to school during the day and work at night.

## Compound Sentences

A compound sentence is a sentence with two independent clauses joined by a comma and a coordinating conjunction. There are seven coordinating conjunctions.

### Coordinating Conjunctions

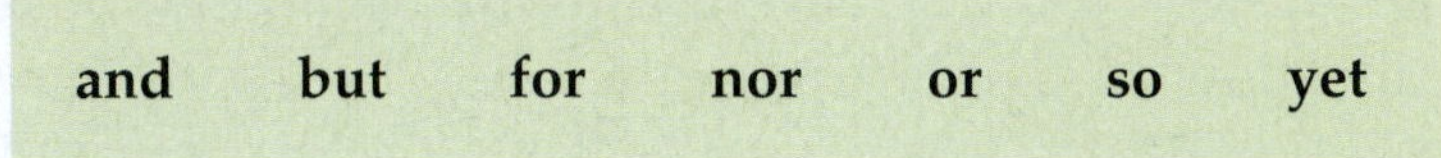

| and | but | for | nor | or | so | yet |
|---|---|---|---|---|---|---|

*And* connects ideas that are equal and similar.

John likes to fish, **and** he often goes fishing.

*But* connects ideas that are equal but different.

The soup was good, **but** it wasn't hot.

*Or* connects equal choices.

We can go to the beach, **or** we can stay home and relax.

*So* connects a reason to a result.

Yesterday was beautiful, **so** we had a picnic by the lake.

## Complex Sentences

A complex sentence is one independent clause and one (or more) dependent clauses, such as time clauses, clauses of reason and condition, and adjective clauses.

### Complex Sentences with Time Clauses

| Time Subordinators | Examples |
|---|---|
| **after** | He goes to school **after** he finishes work. |
| **as soon as** | She felt better **as soon as** she took the medicine. |
| **before** | **Before** you apply to college, you have to take an entrance exam. |
| **since** | It has been a year **since** I left home. |
| **until** | We can't leave the room **until** everyone finishes the test. |
| **when** | **When** you start college, you usually have to take placement tests in math and English. |
| **whenever** | **Whenever** I don't sleep well, I feel sick the next day. |
| **while** | Several overcrowded buses passed **while** they were waiting. |

### Complex Sentences with Clauses of Reason and Condition

| Reason Subordinators | Examples |
|---|---|
| **because** | Jack excels at sports **because** he trains hard. |
| **since** | **Since** she works out daily, Jill is in great condition. |

### Complex Sentences with Clauses of Condition

| Condition Subordinator | Examples |
|---|---|
| **if** | John is unhappy **if** he doesn't get an A in every class.<br>**If** John doesn't get an A in every class, he's unhappy. |

### Complex Sentences with Adjective Clauses

| Relative Pronouns | Examples |
|---|---|
| **who**<br>(people) | People **who** speak several languages are valuable employees.<br>Alfredo, **who** is from Switzerland, speaks three languages. |
| **that**<br>(animals, things, and, in informal English, people) | Yesterday I received an email **that** I did not understand.<br>Tom is the one **that** ran in the marathon. |
| **which**<br>(animals, things) | My new cell phone, **which** I just got yesterday, stopped working today. |

## APPENDIX D TRANSITION SIGNALS

Writers use transition signals to show readers that they are moving from one supporting idea to another. In general, a transition signal shows how the supporting idea it introduces is related to the previous idea. There are several types of transition signals.

| To Show Time Order | |
|---|---|
| First, . . .<br>First of all, . . .<br>Second, . . .<br>Third, . . . | Next, . . .<br>After that, . . .<br>Then . . .<br>Finally, . . . |
| **To Show Listing Order** | |
| First, . . .<br>First of all, . . .<br>Second, . . .<br>Third, . . .<br>In addition, . . . | Also, . . .<br>. . . also . . .<br>. . . , also.<br>Finally, . . . |
| **To Show Space Order** | |
| On the right, . . .<br>On the left, . . .<br>In the center, . . .<br>In the middle, . . .<br>Next to the . . .<br>Beside the . . .<br>Between the . . . | Above the . . .<br>On one side of the . . .<br>On the other side of the . . .<br>Opposite the . . .<br>Near the . . .<br>Under the . . . |
| **To Give a Reason** | |
| The first reason is (that) . . .<br>The second reason is (that) . . .<br>The most important reason is (that) . . . | |
| **To Give an Example** | |
| For example, . . .<br>For instance, . . . | . . . such as __________<br>. . . , such as __________<br>. . . , for example __________<br>. . . , for instance __________ |
| **To Give an Opinion** | |
| In my opinion, . . .<br>In my view, . . .<br>According to __________, . . . | I believe (that) . . .<br>I feel (that) . . .<br>I think (that) . . . |
| **To Add a Conclusion** | |
| In brief, . . .<br>Indeed, . . .<br>In conclusion, . . .<br>In short, . . . | To conclude, . . .<br>To summarize, . . .<br>To sum up, . . .<br>For these reasons, . . . |

## Capitalization

In English, there are many rules for using capital letters. The rules below are some of the most important ones:

| When to Use a Capital Letter | Examples | |
|---|---|---|
| 1. For the first word in a sentence | **M**y neighbor is a mechanic. | |
| 2. For the pronoun *I* | My friends and **I** often study together. | |
| 3. For people's names and their titles | **K**ing **A**bdullah **II** | |
| | **P**resident **L**incoln | |
| | **P**rofessor **P**atrick **J**ones | |
| | **M**r. and **M**rs. **H**arold **S**impson | |
| **Note:** Do not capitalize a title without a name, except when the reference is to a specific person who holds the title. | The **P**resident and **F**irst **L**ady had dinner with the **Q**ueen and her husband last night. | |
| | *Compare with these general references:* | |
| | I've never met a **k**ing or a **p**resident. | |
| | He wants to be a math **p**rofessor. | |
| 4. For nationalities, languages, religions, and ethnic groups | **S**wedish | **E**nglish |
| | **F**arsi | **S**panish |
| | **J**ewish | **M**uslim |
| | **H**ispanic | **N**ative **A**merican |
| 5. For languages or nationalities that are in the name of a school subject or course | **R**ussian | **R**ussian art |
| | **E**nglish | **E**nglish history |
| AND | | |
| names of school courses with numbers | **R**ussian **A**rt 301 | **M**ath 101 |
| | **E**nglish **H**istory 201 | **P**hysics 352 |
| 6. For specific places you can find on a map | **L**ake **T**iticaca | **E**ngland |
| | the **N**orth **P**ole | **F**irst **S**treet |
| | **S**outh **A**merica | **T**imes **S**quare |
| | **A**mazon **R**iver | **N**ew **Y**ork **C**ity |
| 7. For names of specific structures such as buildings, roads, and bridges | the **W**hite **H**ouse | **H**ighway 395 |
| | the **H**ilton **H**otel | **S**tate **R**oute 15 |
| | the **G**reat **W**all | the **B**rooklyn **B**ridge |

*(continued on next page)*

| When to Use a Capital Letter | Examples | |
|---|---|---|
| 8. For names of specific organizations, such as businesses, schools, and clubs | **A**merican **E**xpress<br>**U**nited **N**ations | **Y**ale **U**niversity<br>**O**utdoor **C**lub |
| 9. For names of days of the week, months, holidays, and special time periods<br>**Note**: Do not capitalize the names of seasons. | **M**onday<br>**J**anuary<br>spring<br>summer | **N**ew **Y**ear's **D**ay<br>**R**amadan<br>fall (autumn)<br>winter |
| 10. For geographic areas<br>**Note:** Do not capitalize compass directions. | the **M**iddle **E**ast<br>the **S**outhwest<br>Drive south for two miles and turn west. | **S**outheast **A**sia<br>**E**astern **E**urope |
| 11. For some abbreviations<br>**Note 1:** If a name includes nouns and prepositions, only the first letter of each noun is included in the abbreviation. Notice that prepositions are not capitalized when they are part of a proper noun.<br>**Note 2:** Capitalize only the first letter of the abbreviation of a person's title. | **IBM** **USA** **USC**<br>**CBS** **UN** **UAE**<br>United States <u>of</u> America = **USA**<br>University <u>of</u> Southern California = **USC**<br>**D**r. **M**r. **M**rs. **P**rof. | |
| 12. For each word in a greeting, but only the first word in the closing of a letter or email | **D**ear **S**ir:<br>**T**o **W**hom **I**t **M**ay **C**oncern:<br>**L**ove,<br>**B**est wishes,<br>**V**ery truly yours, | |
| 13. For the titles of movies, TV shows, plays, books, newspapers, and magazines, capitalize the first word and all nouns, pronouns, verbs, adjectives, and adverbs.<br>**Note:** Use *italics* when you write a title on the computer and <u>underline</u> a title when you write it by hand. | Have you seen *Gone with the Wind*?<br>Who wrote *A Raisin in the Sun*?<br>I used to watch *Sesame Street*.<br>He reads <u>The Boston Globe</u> every day. | |

## Punctuation

Correct punctuation helps the reader understand what the writer is trying to say. There are many rules for using commas and quotation marks. Some important ones are below.

| How to Use Commas | Examples |
|---|---|
| **1.** After transition signals (except *then*) and prepositional phrases at the beginning of a sentence | First, carry out the empty bottles and cans.<br>For example, some teachers give pop quizzes.<br>From my window, I have a beautiful view. |
| **2.** Before coordinating conjunctions in a compound sentence | Cook the rice over low heat for twenty minutes, but don't let it burn.<br>Many students work, so they don't have time to do homework. |
| **3.** In a complex sentence, when a dependent (time, reason, or condition) clause comes before an independent clause | Because Mexico City is surrounded by mountains, it has a lot of smog. |
| **4.** To separate items in a series | In our class there are students from Mexico, Korea, Vietnam, Saudi Arabia, and China.<br>Turn left at the stoplight, go one block, and turn right. |
| **5.** To separate thousands, millions, billions, etc. | The trip cost them over $3,000. |
| **Note 1:** Do not use a comma in a number that expresses a year or is part of an address. | 2935 Main Street |
| **Note 2:** Do not use a comma to separate dollars from cents or whole numbers from decimals. Instead, use a decimal point. | $59.95    6⅞ = 6.875<br>$2,999.99    4.5% |
| **6.** To separate the parts of dates and after years in mid-sentence | The third millennium started on January 1, 2001, not on January 1, 2000. |
| **7.** To separate the parts of a U.S. address, except between the state and the zip code. | The address of the Office of Admissions is: 1410 NE Campus Parkway, Seattle, WA 98195. |
| **Note:** When you write an address in a letter or on an envelope, use a comma between the city and state, but do not use a comma at the end of each line. | Office of Admissions<br>1410 NE Campus Parkway<br>Seattle, WA 98195 |

*(continued on next page)*

| How to Use Commas | Examples |
|---|---|
| **8.** After the greeting and closing in an email or a personal letter, and after the closing of an email, a personal letter, or a business letter. | Dear Michiko, Love,<br>Dear Mom, Very truly yours, |
| **Note:** In business letters, a colon (:) is typically used after the greeting. | Dear Ms. Prescott:<br>Dear Sir or Madam:<br>To Whom It May Concern: |

## Quotation Marks

| How to Use Quotation Marks | Examples |
|---|---|
| **1.** Put quotation marks before and after a quotation. | Classmate Sabrina Reyes says, "Mothers of young children should not work because young children need their mothers at home." |
| **Note:** Begin each quotation with a capital letter. | "It's not easy to be a single mother." |
| **2.** Use these rules to separate a reporting phrase from a quotation: | |
| • When the reporting phrase comes before the quotation, follow the reporting phrase with a comma. | **She stated,** "It's not easy to be a single mother." |
| • When the reporting phrase comes after the quotation, put a comma between the last word of the quotation and the quotation mark. | "It's not easy to be a single mother," **she stated.** |
| • When the reporting phrase comes in the middle of a quotation, use two commas to set off the reporting phrase: one inside the quotation mark that ends the first part of the quotation and a second after the reporting phrase. Use a small letter to begin the second part of the quotation. | "It's not easy," **she stated,** "**t**o be a single mother." |
| **3.** Place periods, commas, question marks, and exclamation points inside the end quotation mark. | She said, "Goodbye."<br>"Don't leave so soon," he replied.<br>"Why shouldn't I?" she asked.<br>"Look over there!" he exclaimed. |

## APPENDIX F CORRECTION SYMBOLS

| Symbol | Meaning | Example of Error | Corrected Sentence |
|---|---|---|---|
| p | punctuation | I live, and go to school here (p marks after "live," and after "here") | I live and go to school here. |
| ^ | missing word | I ^ working in a restaurant. (am) | I am working in a restaurant. |
| ___ | rewrite as shown | I go with ~~my some~~ friends. (some of my) | I go with some of my friends. |
| cap | capitalization | It is located at main (cap) and baker (cap) streets (cap) in the City (cap). | It is located at Main and Baker Streets in the city. |
| vt | wrong verb tense | I never work (vt) as a cashier until I get (vt) a job there. | I never worked as a cashier until I got a job there. |
| s/v agr | subject-verb agreement | The manager work (s/v agr) hard. He have (s/v agr) five employees. | The manager works hard. He has five employees. |
| pron agr | pronoun agreement | Everyone works hard at their (pron agr) jobs. | All the employees work hard at their jobs. |
| ⁀ | connect to make one sentence | We work together. So we have become friends. | We work together, so we have become friends. |
| sp | spelling | The maneger (sp) is a woman. | The manager is a woman. |
| sing/pl | singular or plural | She treats her employees like slave (sing/pl). | She treats her employees like slaves. |
| X | unnecessary word | My boss ~~she~~ watches everyone all the time. | My boss watches everyone all the time. |
| wf | wrong word form | Her voice is irritated (wf). | Her voice is irritating. |
| ww | wrong word | The restaurant has great food. Besides (ww), it is always crowded. | The restaurant has great food. Therefore, it is always crowded. |

*(continued on next page)*

| Symbol | Meaning | Example of Error | Corrected Sentence |
|---|---|---|---|
| ref | pronoun reference error | The restaurant's specialty is fish. They (ref) are always fresh. | The restaurant's specialty is fish. It is always fresh. |
| | | The food is delicious. Therefore, it (ref) is always crowded. | The food is delicious. Therefore, the restaurant is always crowded. |
| wo OR ~ | wrong word order | Friday always is our busiest night. | Friday is always our busiest night. |
| ro | run-on sentence | [Lily was fired she is upset.] (ro) | Lily was fired, so she is upset. |
| cs | comma splice | [Lily was fired, she is upset.] (cs) | |
| frag | fragment | She was fired. [Because she was always late.] (frag) | She was fired because she was always late. |
| | | [Is open from 6:00 P.M. until the last customer leaves.] (frag) | The restaurant is open from 6:00 P.M. until the last customer leaves. |
| | | [The employees on time and work hard.] (frag) | The employees are on time and work hard. |
| prep | preposition | We start serving dinner ^ (prep) 6:00 P.M. | We start serving dinner at 6:00 P.M. |
| conj | conjunction | Garlic shrimp, fried clams, ^ (conj) broiled lobster are the most popular dishes. | Garlic shrimp, fried clams, and broiled lobster are the most popular dishes. |
| art | article | Diners in the United States expect ^ (art) glass of water when they first sit down. | Diners in the United States expect a glass of water when they first sit down. |

| Symbol | Meaning | Example of Error | Corrected Sentence |
|---|---|---|---|
| Ⓣ | add a transition | The new employee was Ⓣ careless. She frequently spilled coffee on the table. | The new employee was careless. For example, she frequently spilled coffee on the table. |
| ¶ | start a new paragraph | | |
| nfs/nmp | needs further support/needs more proof. You need to add some specific details (examples, facts, quotations) to support your points. | | |

## CHAPTER 1 PEER REVIEW

**Reader:** ______________________ **Date:** ______________________

1. Does the paragraph give enough information about your classmate's family or family member? ☐ yes ☐ no

   If your answer is no, what else would you like to know?

   ___________________________________________

   ___________________________________________

   ___________________________________________

   ___________________________________________

2. Do you understand everything? ☐ yes ☐ no

   If your answer is no, what part(s) or sentence(s) don't you understand?

   ___________________________________________

   ___________________________________________

   ___________________________________________

   ___________________________________________

3. What do you like the best about this paragraph? Write at least one positive comment here:

   ___________________________________________

   ___________________________________________

   ___________________________________________

   ___________________________________________

## CHAPTER 1 WRITER'S SELF-CHECK

Writer: ______________________ Date: ______________________

**Paragraph Format**

| | | |
|---|---|---|
| My paragraph has a title. | ☐ yes | ☐ no |
| The title is centered. | ☐ yes | ☐ no |
| The first line is indented. | ☐ yes | ☐ no |
| There are margins on both sides of the page. | ☐ yes | ☐ no |
| The paragraph is double-spaced. | ☐ yes | ☐ no |

**Punctuation, Capitalization, and Spelling**

| | | |
|---|---|---|
| I put a period after every sentence. | ☐ yes | ☐ no |
| I used capital letters correctly. | ☐ yes | ☐ no |
| I checked my spelling. | ☐ yes | ☐ no |

**Sentence Structure**

| | | |
|---|---|---|
| Every sentence has at least one subject-verb pair and expresses a complete thought. | ☐ yes | ☐ no |

**Grammar**

Every student has his or her own personal grammar trouble spots. Some students have trouble with verb tenses. For others, articles are the main problem. Some find it hard to know when to use commas. In the next section, write down items that you know are problems for you. Then work on them throughout the course. As time passes, delete items that you have mastered and add new ones that you become aware of.

**Personal Grammar Trouble Spots** (verb tense, articles, word order, etc.) — **Number found and corrected**

I checked my paragraph for:

- ______________________________ ____________
- ______________________________ ____________
- ______________________________ ____________

## CHAPTER 2 PEER REVIEW

**Reader:** ______________________ **Date:** ______________________

1. How many main points does the writer make? Number: ____

2. Does the writer introduce each main point with a listing-order transition signal? ☐ yes ☐ no

   Which signals does the writer use? Write them here:

   ______________________________________________

3. Does each main point have a detail? ☐ yes ☐ no

   Write one detail that you especially like:

   ______________________________________________

4. Do you understand everything? ☐ yes ☐ no

   If your answer is no, what part(s) or sentence(s) don't you understand?

   ______________________________________________

   ______________________________________________

   ______________________________________________

   ______________________________________________

   ______________________________________________

5. What do you like the best about this paragraph? Write at least one positive comment here:

   ______________________________________________

   ______________________________________________

   ______________________________________________

   ______________________________________________

   ______________________________________________

## CHAPTER 2 WRITER'S SELF-CHECK

**Writer:** ______________________ **Date:** ______________________

**Paragraph Format**

My paragraph looks like the model on page 38. ☐ yes ☐ no

**Organization**

My paragraph begins with a topic sentence and ends with a concluding sentence. ☐ yes ☐ no

My topic sentence has both a topic and a controlling idea. ☐ yes ☐ no

I use listing order to organize my paragraph. ☐ yes ☐ no

I use listing-order transition signals to introduce each main point. ☐ yes ☐ no

**Punctuation, Capitalization, and Spelling**

I put a period after every sentence. ☐ yes ☐ no

I used capital letters correctly. ☐ yes ☐ no

I checked my spelling. ☐ yes ☐ no

**Sentence Structure**

I wrote at least three compound sentences. ☐ yes ☐ no

I checked my paragraph for run-on and comma splice errors. ☐ yes ☐ no

**Personal Grammar Trouble Spots** (verb tense, articles, word order, etc.) — **Number found and corrected**

I checked my paragraph for:

- ______________________ ______
- ______________________ ______
- ______________________ ______

## CHAPTER 3 PEER REVIEW

**Reader:** ______________________ **Date:** ______________________

1. What is the topic of this paragraph?

   How to ______________________

   ______________________

2. Does the paragraph begin with a topic sentence? ☐ yes ☐ no

   Copy the topic sentence here: ______________________

   ______________________

3. Do you understand everything? ☐ yes ☐ no

   If your answer is no, what part(s) or sentence(s) don't you understand?

   ______________________

   ______________________

   ______________________

   ______________________

   ______________________

4. Does the writer use transition signals (*first*, *next*, and so on) to help you understand each step? ☐ yes ☐ no

5. What do you like the best about this paragraph? Write at least one positive comment here:

   ______________________

   ______________________

   ______________________

   ______________________

   ______________________

## CHAPTER 3 WRITER'S SELF-CHECK

**Writer:** ______________________ **Date:** ______________________

### Paragraph Format

My paragraph looks like the model on page 74. ☐ yes ☐ no

### Organization

My paragraph begins with a "how to" topic sentence. ☐ yes ☐ no

The steps are in time order or listing order. ☐ yes ☐ no

I used time-order or listing-order transition signals with some of the steps. ☐ yes ☐ no

### Punctuation, Capitalization, and Spelling

I put a period after every sentence. ☐ yes ☐ no

I used capital letters correctly. ☐ yes ☐ no

I checked my spelling. ☐ yes ☐ no

### Sentence Structure

Every sentence has at least one subject-verb pair and expresses a complete thought. ☐ yes ☐ no

I wrote at least three complex sentences, and I punctuated them correctly. ☐ yes ☐ no

I checked for run-ons, comma splices, and fragments. ☐ yes ☐ no

| **Personal Grammar Trouble Spots** (verb tense, articles, word order, etc.) | **Number found and corrected** |
|---|---|
| I checked my paragraph for: | |
| • ______________________ | ____________ |
| • ______________________ | ____________ |
| • ______________________ | ____________ |

## CHAPTER 4 PEER REVIEW

**Reader:** ______________________ **Date:** ______________________

1. What is the topic of this paragraph?

______________________________________________________________

______________________________________________________________

2. Does the paragraph begin with a topic sentence? ☐ yes ☐ no

Copy the topic sentence here: ______________________________

______________________________________________________________

3. Do you understand everything? ☐ yes ☐ no

If your answer is no, what part(s) or sentence(s) don't you understand?

______________________________________________________________

______________________________________________________________

______________________________________________________________

______________________________________________________________

4. Does the writer use space order? ☐ yes ☐ no

Write three space-order signals that the writer used:

______________________________________________________________

5. Does the writer use adjectives in the description? ☐ yes ☐ no

Write three phrases with adjectives that the writer used:

______________________________________________________________

6. What do you like the best about this paragraph? Write at least one positive comment here:

______________________________________________________________

______________________________________________________________

______________________________________________________________

______________________________________________________________

## CHAPTER 4 WRITER'S SELF-CHECK

**Writer:** ______________________ **Date:** ______________________

**Paragraph Format**

My paragraph looks like the model on page 111. ☐ yes ☐ no

**Organization**

I included a topic sentence and a concluding sentence. ☐ yes ☐ no

I used space order to organize my description. ☐ yes ☐ no

I used lots of details to help my reader "see" the room. ☐ yes ☐ no

**Grammar**

I used adjectives to describe different objects in the room. ☐ yes ☐ no

I put cumulative adjectives in the correct order. ☐ yes ☐ no

I used commas between coordinate adjectives. ☐ yes ☐ no

**Punctuation, Capitalization, and Spelling**

I put a period after every sentence. ☐ yes ☐ no

I used capital letters correctly. ☐ yes ☐ no

I checked my spelling. ☐ yes ☐ no

**Sentence Structure**

I checked that each sentence has at least one subject-verb pair and expresses a complete thought. ☐ yes ☐ no

I used a mix of simple, compound, and complex sentences. ☐ yes ☐ no

I began some sentences with a prepositional phrase. ☐ yes ☐ no

I checked for run-ons, comma splices, and fragments. ☐ yes ☐ no

| **Personal Grammar Trouble Spots** (verb tense, articles, word order, etc.) | **Number found and corrected** |
|---|---|
| I checked my paragraph for: | |
| • ______________________ | __________ |
| • ______________________ | __________ |
| • ______________________ | __________ |

## CHAPTER 5 PEER REVIEW

**Reader:** ______________________ **Date:** ______________________

1. How many reasons does the writer give? Number: ____

2. Does the writer introduce each reason with a transition signal? ☐ yes ☐ no

   Which transition signals does the writer use?

   ______________________________________________________________

   ______________________________________________________________

3. Does each reason have an example? ☐ yes ☐ no

   Write one example that you especially like:

   ______________________________________________________________

   ______________________________________________________________

4. Do you understand everything? ☐ yes ☐ no

   If your answer is no, what part(s) or sentence(s) don't you understand?

   ______________________________________________________________

   ______________________________________________________________

   ______________________________________________________________

   ______________________________________________________________

   ______________________________________________________________

5. What do you like the best about this paragraph? Write at least one positive comment here:

   ______________________________________________________________

   ______________________________________________________________

   ______________________________________________________________

   ______________________________________________________________

   ______________________________________________________________

## CHAPTER 5 WRITER'S SELF-CHECK

**Writer:** ______________________ **Date:** ______________________

**Paragraph Format**

My paragraph looks like the model on page 140. ☐ yes ☐ no

**Organization**

My paragraph begins with a topic sentence and ends with a concluding sentence. ☐ yes ☐ no

I used listing order to organize the reasons. ☐ yes ☐ no

I used transition signals to introduce each reason. ☐ yes ☐ no

I used at least one example or other specific detail for each reason. ☐ yes ☐ no

**Punctuation, Capitalization, and Spelling**

I checked punctuation, capitalization, and spelling. ☐ yes ☐ no

**Sentence Structure**

I checked that each sentence has at least one subject-verb pair and expresses a complete thought. ☐ yes ☐ no

I used a mix of simple, compound, and complex sentences. ☐ yes ☐ no

I checked for run-ons, comma splices, and fragments. ☐ yes ☐ no

| **Personal Grammar Trouble Spots** (verb tense, articles, word order, etc.) | **Number found and corrected** |
|---|---|
| I checked my paragraph for: | |
| • ______________________ | __________ |
| • ______________________ | __________ |
| • ______________________ | __________ |

## CHAPTER 6 PEER REVIEW

**Reader:** ____________________ **Date:** ____________________

**1.** How many reasons does the writer give? Number: ____

**2.** Does the writer introduce each reason with a transition signal? ☐ yes ☐ no

Which transition signals does the writer use?

______________________________________________

______________________________________________

**3.** Does each reason have supporting facts? ☐ yes ☐ no

**4.** Does the writer use at least one quotation? ☐ yes ☐ no

**5.** Do you understand everything? ☐ yes ☐ no

If your answer is no, what part(s) or sentence(s) don't you understand?

______________________________________________

______________________________________________

______________________________________________

______________________________________________

______________________________________________

**6.** What do you like the best about this paragraph? Write at least one positive comment here:

______________________________________________

______________________________________________

______________________________________________

______________________________________________

______________________________________________

## CHAPTER 6 WRITER'S SELF-CHECK

**Writer:** ______________________ **Date:** ______________________

**Paragraph Format**

My paragraph looks like the model on page 168. ☐ yes ☐ no

**Organization**

My paragraph begins with a clear opinion topic sentence. ☐ yes ☐ no

I used transition signals to introduce each reason. ☐ yes ☐ no

I used one or two supporting details for each reason. ☐ yes ☐ no

I used at least one quotation. ☐ yes ☐ no

**Punctuation, Capitalization, and Spelling**

I checked punctuation, capitalization, and spelling. ☐ yes ☐ no

**Sentence Structure**

I checked that each sentence has at least one subject-verb pair and expresses a complete thought. ☐ yes ☐ no

I used a mix of simple, compound, and complex sentences. ☐ yes ☐ no

I wrote at least two sentences with adjective clauses. ☐ yes ☐ no

I checked for run-ons, comma splices, and fragments. ☐ yes ☐ no

**Personal Grammar Trouble Spots** **Number found and corrected**
(verb tense, articles, word order, etc.)

I checked my paragraph for:

- ______________________ ____________
- ______________________ ____________
- ______________________ ____________

# INDEX

## P



## Q



## R



## S

## T



## U



## V



## W

# CREDITS

**Photo credits:**

**Page 1** Chris Curtis/Shutterstock; **p. 4** LoopAll/Fotolia; **p. 17** Continua/Shutterstock; **p. 19** Allstar Picture Library/Alamy; **p. 21** Creator: BlueMoon Stock/Alamy; **p. 25** Josh Thompson/Cal Sport Media/ Newscom; **p. 34** Robert Matton AB/Alamy; **p. 40** LoopAll/Fotolia; **p. 42** Monkey Business Images/Shutterstock; **p. 47** LoopAll/Fotolia; **p. 52** LoopAll/Fotolia; **p. 59** Anita P Peppers/Fotolia; **p. 60** Gary Conner/Getty Images; **p. 65** Alexander Raths/Shutterstock; **p. 70** nyul/Fotolia; **p. 72** haveseen/Fotolia; **p. 73** The Dealers/Shutterstock; **p. 80** Ivelin Ivanov/Fotolia; **p. 81** (top) Radosław Brzozo/Fotolia, (bottom) Agencja FREE/Alamy; **p. 82** paylessimages/Fotolia; **p. 94** (1) Malyshev Maksim/Shutterstock, (2) AVD/Fotolia, (3) oksana2010/Shutterstock, (4) HelleM/Shutterstock; **p. 106** Denis Kuvaev/Shutterstock; **p. 122** maxik/Shutterstock; **p. 136** (top) Erkki & Hanna/Shutterstock, (bottom) Eduardo Rivero/Fotolia; **p. 138** Andres Rodriguez/Fotolia; **p. 145** Tetra Images/Alamy; **p. 152** OLIVER KILLIG/EPA/Newscom; **p. 155** michaeljung/Shutterstock; **p. 164** The Bridgeman Art Library/Getty Images; **p. 166** Simone van den Berg/Fotolia; **p. 186** pryzmat/Shutterstock; **p. 187** Jim West/Alamy

**Illustration credits:**

**Steve Attoe:** p. 100; **Greg Rebis:** pp. 108, 109, 116; **Steve Schulman:** p. 2